DISCOVERING
The Boyne Valley

DISCOVERING
The Boyne Valley

NOEL FRENCH

MERCIER PRESS
IRISH PUBLISHER - IRISH STORY

The passage tomb at Knowth.
© *iStockphoto*

MERCIER PRESS
Cork
www.mercierpress.ie

ISBN: 978 1 78117 521 7

10 9 8 7 6 5 4 3 2 1

A CIP record for this title is available from the British Library

Printed and bound in the EU.

Contents

Slane Castle.

Acknowledgements

I would like to thank the following for allowing me to use their images in this book: Aubrey Martin: Hill of Ward, Loughcrew, Mellifont and Tara; Joe Conlon: excavations on Tlachtga; Seamus Farrelly: Pierce Brosnan; John Scarry: Newgrange, Knowth and Loughcrew. Unless credited otherwise, the images are from the author's own collection.

I would also like to thank Fechin Heery, Malachy Hand, Michael Fox, Derek Smith, Michael Farry, Danny Cusack, Paschal Marry, John Devitt, Ethna Cantwell, Vincent Mulvaney and Conor Brady for their help with the content of the book, and Wendy Logue for her work in editing the book.

The author's royalties for this book are being donated in their entirety to the Meath branch of the Alzheimer's Society of Ireland in memory of my mother, who suffered from that disease.

The walls and Dublingate
of Trim Castle.

Introduction

The Boyne Valley is one of Ireland's most magical and important historical areas, as well as a place of myths and legends. The stunning landscape of the valley rises up around the famous River Boyne and runs through County Meath, which proudly boasts of being the heritage capital of Ireland, and County Louth, the land of legends. It is a relatively small area to explore, allowing you to discover many of the major attractions in a day. This book focuses on the highlights of the area, although there are many more minor sites along the way.

The rich valley is home to a range of heritage sites and monuments. Places like Newgrange, Tara, Kells and the site of the Battle of the Boyne are well known nationally and internationally, but there are other sites, such as Trim, Loughcrew, Monasterboice and Mellifont, which would be major attractions in their own right were they not overshadowed by the more recognised locations. Moreover, the towns of the area, including Navan and Drogheda, host their own attractions.

The historical significance of the area began over 5,000 years ago, when the world-famous tombs at Brú na Bóinne were constructed.

County Meath is also celebrated as the Royal County, the place from which the high kings of Ireland reigned from their ritual seat on Tara, and it was the Boyne Valley where St Patrick first preached the Christian faith in Ireland, lighting the Paschal fire on the Hill of Slane.

Following Patrick's activities, monastic schools of learning were quickly established. One of them, Kells, is famed throughout the world for its high crosses and illuminated manuscripts. Viking raiders frequently visited this fertile valley to prey on the easy pickings that the rich monastic settlements offered. In the twelfth century their descendants, the Normans, started construction on what would become the largest castle in Ireland, at Trim. These talented builders erected a number of castles, churches, monasteries and crosses along the banks of the Boyne and its tributary the Blackwater, many of which are still part of the landscape.

Another (even less welcome) visitor to the Boyne Valley was Oliver Cromwell, who wreaked such havoc in Drogheda that he is still a figure of hate in today's Ireland. Less than fifty years later, King William and King James battled it out for the British throne at Oldbridge, in what is now known as the Battle of the Boyne. Following 'King Billy's' victory, new conquerors came and the big houses and the mansions of the landlords now sit prettily above the river.

The Irish people long sought independence from their British overlords and in 1798 a small battle took place at Tara as part of the United Irish rebellion of that year. Tara was also the site of a monster meeting held by Daniel O'Connell, the Liberator, in his attempt to have the Act of Union of 1801 repealed.

This is just a small indication of the central role this landscape has played in Ireland's history over the millennia. It is a role that fascinates me and I have spent the last forty years in the valley. I never tire of revisiting the various sites and although I cannot physically go back in time, my mind travels back when I walk the ground that people have inhabited for over 5,000 years. I hope you get as much enjoyment from visiting these places as I do.

Information with regard to opening hours, admission fees and booking is correct at the time of publishing, but that may change, so it is advisable to check with each site.

Finally, a word of advice: try to go off peak, as when the crowds are smaller you get time to enjoy the sites more comfortably. Also, during off peak times it is usually the experienced guides who are on site, and they have years of knowledge which they love to share with visitors.

King William of Orange from a mural in Belfast

The Battle of the Boyne

The Battle of the Boyne was contested between the forces of William of Orange and James II in July 1690, on a site that sprawls over a wide area west of the town of Drogheda. This 300-year-old conflict continues to impact on current-day events in modern Ireland, retaining huge symbolic importance in Northern Ireland, where it is celebrated by the Orange Order every 12 July. It was also the last time two crowned kings of England, Scotland and Ireland faced each other on a battlefield. But the battle was about more than the fate of the islands of Britain and Ireland – it was a European battle being fought on Irish soil. At stake was not only the British throne, but also French dominance in Europe.

King James II had succeeded to the throne of Britain and Ireland in 1685. He sought to restore the Catholic religion as the state religion and also the absolute power of the king to overrule parliament. Less than forty years previously his father, King Charles I, had lost his head because he wished to be an absolute ruler. Despite this, the establishment in England seemed willing to tolerate James' rule as long as his successor would be one of his Protestant daughters: Mary, who was married to her first cousin, William of Orange, or Anne.

Then, in 1673, James married for a second time. His bride, Mary of Modena, was twenty-five years younger than him and a devout Roman Catholic. In 1687 Queen Mary became pregnant and in June 1688 gave birth to a healthy boy, James Francis Edward Stuart. This provided for a Catholic succession, a state of affairs that was unacceptable to the Protestant parliament. Rumours soon arose about the birth: it was alleged that the baby had been stillborn and was replaced by a healthy baby smuggled into the birthing chamber in a bedpan. Whatever the validity of these rumours, the English establishment reacted to the birth by inviting William and Mary to rule Britain instead of James.

In November 1688 William landed in England and was greeted warmly. James, who had been preparing for the inevitable fight with William, found his army depleted by desertions to the other side. The final straw came when he discovered that his second daughter, Anne, had also deserted his cause, and he fled the country.

James sought refuge with his old ally, Louis XIV of France, who saw an opportunity to strike at his enemy William through Ireland. Louis had been attempting to expand his territory into the Dutch Republic for some time, but so far had been successfully opposed by William and his forces. The French king gave officers and arms to James, who saw Ireland as a back door to regain his kingdom: first Ireland, then Scotland and finally England. His Irish supporters would have been happy to see him as king of Ireland only.

James landed at Kinsale in March 1689. A year later the Jacobite army was strengthened by 7,000 French regulars, although Louis demanded that over 5,000 Irish troops go to France immediately in return. In June 1690 William came in person to Ireland, landing at Carrickfergus, on the north shore of Belfast Lough. He led a large army composed of, among others, Dutch, Germans and Huguenot French, as well as English, Irish and Scots, who were far better trained and equipped than James' troops.

James decided to block William's advance towards Dublin at the River Boyne near Drogheda. His army occupied the town and the Oldbridge area to its west. On the evening of 30 June William's army began to appear on the north bank of the river, where they set up camp. At the same time, from a tent beside the ruins of a small medieval church on Donore Hill, which overlooks the Boyne from the south bank, James oversaw the disposition of his troops. William controlled an army of 36,000 men, while James had a force of 25,000, making this the largest number of soldiers ever deployed on an Irish battlefield.

Donore Church, where King James based his command.

On the evening before the battle William surveyed his troop movements from horseback. A Jacobite gunner seized the opportunity to shoot a cannon ball at him – it grazed William's right shoulder. A little bit to one side and the end result could have been very different.

For the battle James placed his army in a box of land surrounded on three sides by the Boyne, the north bank of which at this point is bordered by high ground, meaning he could not see how William was setting out his forces. In contrast, the gently sloping south bank allowed William to see the exact disposition of James' troops.

At his council of war the night before the battle, William had decided to dispatch 10,000 of his forces upriver to attack King James' forces from the west. James, anticipating just such a flanking movement, held half his force in reserve on his west flank to face this threat. On the day of the battle these forces came face to face across a deep, swampy ravine. Neither seemed interested in crossing the ravine and thereby putting themselves at the disadvantage of having to fight uphill out of a steep valley. This resulted in a stand-off between these two sections. It also meant that a large force of Jacobite troops was effectively kept out of the battle by a smaller detachment of Williamites.

The main Williamite force began wading across the river on the morning of the battle at the ford of Oldbridge, making their attack down a narrow valley now named King William's Glen. Overcoming stiff resistance from repeated charges of King James' Irish cavalry, the Williamites gained the south bank of the river. The Protestant French regiment fighting for William was urged to attack their compatriot Catholics with the cry of 'Onward, those are your enemies.'

When the infantry attack across the Boyne stalled shortly after noon because of attacks by the Irish cavalry, William personally crossed the river and led his cavalry squadrons up Donore Hill. With both armies wearing similar clothing, a confusing fight ensued, which almost led to William's death as one of his men pointed a pistol at him, to which he shouted, 'What, are you angry with your friends?'

William's numerical supremacy in both forces and artillery carried the day. The battle was not a massive engagement by international standards: about 1,000 Jacobites and 500 Williamites were killed.

When James saw the battle was going against him he fled to Dublin. The Jacobite army pulled back south to Duleek and crossed the Nanny river, after which it scattered. As James entered the gates of Dublin, the lord lieutenant's wife, Lady Tyrconnel, welcomed him. He declared, 'Madam, your countrymen run well' – in other words, according to James the Irish had run from the battle. She replied, 'Sire, you must not be a bad runner yourself as I see you have won the race.' James was one of the first from the battle to reach Dublin, from where he fled to Waterford and thence back to France.

William did not reach Dublin for another five days. Why was he seemingly reluctant to pursue his defeated foe? Presumably because not only was James a king, but he was also William's uncle and father-in-law. William's mother was James' sister. To capture James would have left William in a predicament, because if he executed him, he would have been seen to be condoning the execution of kings and such an action would leave open the possibility that someone could use execution as a means of removing William himself in the future.

The Boyne was truly a European battle, with both armies filled with Irish, English, Scots, French and also, on the Williamite side, Dutch, Danish and German soldiers. Confusion reigned during the battle as there were no standard uniforms and many on both sides wore very similar clothes. Although today green is seen as the colour of the Irish nationalist, William's men wore a green cockade or green leaves in their hats (not orange!). The Jacobite army took the colour white as their colour, from the French *fleur de lis*.

The battle was fought on 1 July, yet today it is remembered on 12 July. At that time Britain and the Protestant world were still using the old Roman calendar devised by Julius Caesar. They refused to adopt the more correct Gregorian calendar because it had been devised by a Catholic pope. In 1752, when Britain finally adopted the Gregorian changes, it had to skip ten days in September in order to make their calendar accurate. This led to riots in London by protestors who wanted these days back, as they believed their lives were being shortened by ten days. So the year 1752 in Britain had only 355 days. Even so, this new calendar meant that the Boyne should be celebrated on 11 July, so it is still commemorated on the wrong date. The use of 12 July actually comes from the day originally commemorated by Williamites, that of the Battle of Aughrim in County Galway, the decisive battle of the war between supporters of James and William in Ireland which occurred on 12 July 1691 (in the old calendar).

Despite what commemorations today may suggest, the Battle of the Boyne was not a straight Catholic versus Protestant battle. There were Protestants and Catholics on both sides, but William's side was predominantly Protestant and James' predominately Catholic. Interestingly, the pope backed the Protestant King William. In this case politics won out over religious beliefs. At that time Pope Alexander VIII and the Papal States were part of a Grand Alliance seeking to limit the expansion of France, with one of the areas of contention being the northern states of Italy ruled by the pope. Hailing the success of William at the Boyne, Alexander VIII ordered the bells of the Vatican to be rung in celebration. Another leader of the Grand Alliance, the Catholic Austrian Emperor Leopold, had high masses said on news of the victory at the Boyne.

An interesting addendum to Pope Alexander's support of William comes from more recent times. A painting of William arriving in Ireland was purchased sight unseen by the Unionist government of Northern Ireland for the new Stormont parliament in 1933, but when it arrived it was discovered that it included the figure of the pope blessing William's endeavour. As a result the painting was first vandalised and then hidden away. It is now on display in the waiting area outside the speaker's office.

The colour of the horse William rode on the day is traditionally deemed to be white, but this may not be true, as a white horse would have stood out in the countryside and made its rider an easier target. William initially rode a dark horse at the Boyne before the poor animal sank to its haunches in riverside mud, and he changed horse at least once on the battle site whilst fording the river at Oldbridge.

Despite their defeat at the Battle of the Boyne, James' Irish forces fought on for another year. It was not until the Battle of Aughrim that the Jacobite forces were decisively beaten. Following this defeat James' supporters agreed to the Treaty of Limerick, which allowed his soldiers free passage to France, while those who remained in Ireland were guaranteed their religious freedoms and the right to their estates or to carry on their trades or professions. The treaty was a very fair settlement, but hardly had the ink dried on the signatures and the Irish soldiers departed

Oldbridge House, now the Battle of the Boyne visitor centre.
© *Shutterstock*

for the continent, before the Protestant parliament commenced passing anti-Catholic laws.

It was the later Orange Order that popularised the connection of the Boyne with 12 July. The Order grew out of sectarian conflict in the late eighteenth century and was founded in 1795, with the first meeting of the Grand Orange Lodge held in Dawson Street, Dublin in 1798. The Orange celebrations include huge bonfires, parades and religious ceremonies. The parades have led to conflict as the Order wishes to march the 'Queen's highway' on its traditional routes, even if the residents of the route are now mainly nationalists. Only one Orange parade takes place in the Republic, in Rossnowlagh, County Donegal.

With the state's purchase of Oldbridge House and part of the battle site, a decision was made to develop a visitor attraction and presentation that would commemorate the battle and at the same time be a place of peace and reconciliation between the unionist and nationalist communities on the island. At the opening of the Battle of the Boyne visitor centre in 2008 the then Northern Ireland First Minister, Rev. Ian Paisley, declared, 'To the bad old days there can be no turning back. The killing times must end for ever and no tolerance must be given to those who advocate their return. A strong dedication to peace and an intolerance of murder must drive us forward.' Then Irish Taoiseach Bertie Ahern said, 'In recent years, many of us from the nationalist tradition have come to a greater appreciation of the history, traditions and identity of those of you from the unionist tradition with whom we share this island … We need – all of us – to understand our shared history if we are to build a shared future. The principles and ideals that we hold dear are the same – liberty and equality, democracy and peace. If we hold fast to those shared ideals, our children will have an inheritance to treasure.' Using original seventeenth-century swords, the Taoiseach and First Minister jointly cut the ribbon at the site.

Oldbridge House, which houses the new visitor centre, was once home to John Coddington, whose father, Captain Dixie Coddington, was on the staff of William III at the Battle of the Boyne. John purchased Oldbridge from the Earl of Drogheda in 1729. Dixie Coddington is also alleged to have been the six-time great-grandfather of American Senator John McCain, who ran against Barack Obama in the US presidential election of 2008.

The Battle of the Boyne visitor centre is open all year round. An admission charge applies to the display and audio-visual. There is free access to the battle site, parklands and the formal walled gardens. There is a large car park and tea pavilion. Regular weaponry displays take place during the summer months.

Bective Abbey and
the River Boyne.

Bective Abbey

Bective Abbey was established on the banks of the River Boyne in 1147, although nothing remains of the original monastic foundation. The earliest part of the present range of buildings dates to the thirteenth century, including the chapter house (where meetings would have been held), which is part of the west range of buildings. Most of the remaining ruins date to the fifteenth and sixteenth centuries. At the centre of the complex is a fine monastic cloister, a covered passageway that surrounded an enclosed courtyard. One of the pillars of the cloister bears a figure, possibly an abbot, carrying a crozier.

Bective Abbey was the first daughter house of Mellifont Abbey. Mellifont was the first Cistercian monastery in Ireland, founded in 1142, and within a decade it had four 'daughter' houses, dependent houses where the 'mother' house retains ultimate authority over the community. Bective was founded by Murchadh Ua Máel Sechlainn, the king of Meath. Dedicated to the Virgin Mary, the monastery was assigned the name Bective from *De Beatitudine* or *Beatitudo Dei*, meaning the blessedness of God.

Cistercian monasteries were usually located in isolated rural settings and sited along rivers. The Cistercians were industrious farmers, with cereals, cattle and sheep being produced. Fisheries were developed and mills, bakeries and other local industries initiated by the monks at Bective.

The site was located in the centre of the territory of Midhe, which was granted to Hugh de Lacy by King Henry II in 1172, following the arrival of the Anglo-Normans in Ireland, although there is no surviving record of de Lacy ever making a donation to the monastery. De Lacy was assassinated by an Irishman called O'Kearney at Durrow in 1186 when he was overseeing the construction of a castle on that site. According to Irish sources of the time, this was in revenge for taking stones from the monastery at Durrow. De Lacy's head and body were recovered from the Irish nine years later and his body was interred at Bective, while his head was buried at St Thomas' Abbey in Dublin. The fact that

Bective Abbey.

de Lacy's body initially came to Bective is an indication of its high status at the time. Religious communities were anxious to acquire the bodies of their founders or distinguished benefactors, possibly due to the financial gains that could be had from hosting the remains, and so Bective's claim to de Lacy was challenged by St Thomas', where the remains of de Lacy's first wife also lay. In 1205 judges appointed by Pope Innocent III decreed in favour of removal of de Lacy's body to St Thomas', where it was finally buried alongside that of his wife.

This was not the only colourful episode in Bective's history. In 1217 the abbot was accused of participating in a 'riot' at Jerpoint Abbey, County Kilkenny, and was further charged with imprisoning a man in a tree stump until the man died.

In the mid-fourteenth century the Black Death, which ravaged Europe, halved the numbers of monks in Bective, while lay numbers were also greatly reduced.

In 1386 men of Irish birth were effectively barred from entering the monastery in order to ensure that it remained loyal to the English king. Bective was on the border area between the Pale (the relatively small area of land centred on Dublin that was controlled by the English at this time) and the uncivilised and rebellious Irish who inhabited the rest of the country. The large fortified tower that still partially survives was constructed as protection from Irish attacks into the Pale. Rebuilding at Bective in the late fifteenth century was also prompted by the need to adapt the buildings for the smaller numbers of monks it now housed.

Bective Abbey was closed in 1536 during the Dissolution of the Monasteries by Henry VIII and the estate was gifted to a loyal civil servant. Lord Dunsany wrote that when the monks left Bective to go to Trim they took up half a mile of road. The new owner, Thomas Agard, began the process of converting the complex into a great sprawling Tudor manor house, with the insertion of new fireplaces, chimneys and large stone windows. The cloister became an internal courtyard and the refectory was turned into a Great Hall. The estate passed through the hands of various civil servants, none of whom had the time to pay any great attention to its development, and it eventually fell into ruin.

In more recent times Bective Abbey enjoyed a short period of celebrity when it was chosen to be the location for two scenes in *Braveheart,* the well-known movie starring Mel Gibson and filmed in Ireland during the summer of 1994. The abbey served as the courtyard of Edward I's castle and was also used to represent the dungeons in which Wallace is imprisoned.

A little downriver from the abbey is Bective House, once the home of John Watson. Watson, one of the most famous equestrian sportsmen in Ireland, is recognised as the 'Father of Polo' as he formulated a set of fundamental rules for the game. The name Bective is also recalled in the first book of short stories by local writer Mary Lavin, *Tales from Bective Bridge.*

Near the abbey, on the south side of the river, is Balsoon House, which is associated with the Ussher family. James Ussher was rector of the nearby parish of Assey from 1611 to 1626. He became Archbishop of Armagh and Primate of All Ireland in 1625 but is most famous for establishing the time of Creation as around 6 p.m. on 22 October 4004 BC. Many older Bibles have this chronology as a side listing on their pages and its accuracy is still accepted as fact by some modern-day creationists.

Bective Abbey is open all year round with no admission charge. A car park ensures safe parking. It is signposted from the R161 between Trim and Navan and is also a convenient stopping point if you are visiting Tara and Trim. The ruins provide a maze of passageways with dead ends and interrupted staircases, and are perfect for a family picnic.

The exterior of St Peter's Catholic Church.

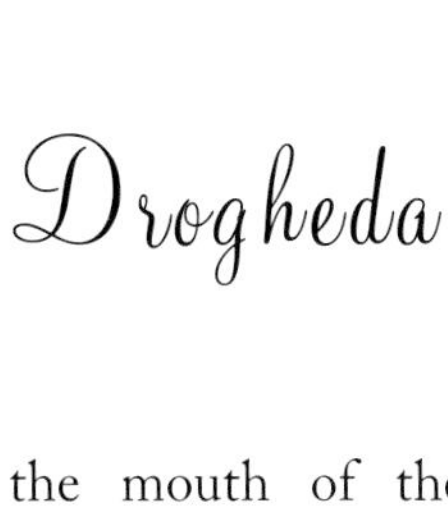

Drogheda

Located at the mouth of the River Boyne, Drogheda's name is derived from the Irish *Droichead Átha*, meaning bridge of the ford. The Anglo-Normans created two separate towns on either side of the river in the late twelfth century. The two towns were (and still are) in different church dioceses, Meath on the south side and Armagh on the north, and they had separate corporations, taxes, tariffs and landing charges. The commercial rivalry between the two even led to loss of life as each town sought to undercut the other in order to gain a greater share of the local market. The historian John D'Alton records that, 'In their contests blood was often shed, and many lives lost, especially upon one occasion when the bridge became the scene of a sanguinary engagement between the conflicting parties.' Finally, in 1412, the two communities were convinced by Fr Philip Bennet, a local monk, to unite and seek a single charter from the king, in which they were successful.

Drogheda developed as a thriving major port in medieval times. In 1494 Poyning's Law, which made the Irish parliament subject to the English crown and parliament, was passed at a parliament held in Drogheda and dominated by supporters of the crown. The purpose of this law was to curb the independence of Ireland's parliament and it continued to do so until the end of the eighteenth century.

In recent centuries Drogheda's importance as a port has waned, but it has become a significant manufacturing centre. In the 1930s the Boyne Road Cement Factory was constructed east of the town on the River Boyne. The large, open quarry northwest of the town was the source of stone for this plant. In 1977 a new cement factory opened at Platin, west of Drogheda, and the old factory was taken over by Premier Periclase, which produces magnesia products from seawater and limestone.

There are two bridges in Drogheda that all visitors will notice. The elegant viaduct which carries the Dublin to Belfast railway across the Boyne estuary was completed in 1855 and has a span of 430 metres. Upriver, the Mary McAleese Boyne Valley Bridge, which carries the M1 motorway north, is named after our second female president and was opened in June 2003.

Probably the most hated name in Drogheda, if not all of Ireland, is that of Oliver Cromwell, Lord Protector of England. His attack on Drogheda on 11 September 1649, when his army broke into the town and slaughtered its defenders, was perhaps the most ferocious sacking of a town in Irish history. Drogheda was held by Royalist forces under Governor Arthur Aston when Cromwell and his forces laid siege to the town in early September. The siege lasted two days before Cromwell's cannons made a breach in the walls. As Cromwell observed the attack on the breach and saw how many of his soldiers were dying, he gave orders to take no prisoners. He reported back to parliament that 'that night they put to the sword about two thousand men'.

There has been, and continues to be, controversy in relation to this action. On one side the story is that all the inhabitants, including innocent men, women and children, were slaughtered, and certainly there is evidence of civilian deaths. On the other side it is asserted that the majority of those killed were soldiers who had caused unnecessary casualties in the Cromwellian army by pointlessly holding out against the siege. What is certain is that the massacre at Drogheda became the symbol for the cruelty of the Cromwellian war in Ireland. What happened there was by all accounts a savage affair, but it was meant to be a deterrent, to discourage future resistance from other towns. The ferocity of Cromwell's army in Drogheda may or may not have succeeded in shortening the Cromwellian war in Ireland, but it certainly shocked both Royalist and Irish Catholic opinion.

For the 200 soldiers who surrendered, Cromwell's orders decreed that 'their officers were [to be killed by being] knocked on the head, and every tenth man of the soldiers killed, and the rest shipped to Barbados'. Governor Aston, who had lost part of a leg in a riding accident years previously and had a wooden one fitted, was apparently beaten to death with his own wooden leg. Cromwell's soldiers had heard a rumour that it contained gold and when it was discovered to be plain wood, Aston suffered a gruesome fate. Thousands of military prisoners from Cromwell's Irish campaign were sold in perpetuity to plantation-owners in Barbados and other islands in the Caribbean to work in the fields, effectively as slaves. Their descendants continue to reside in the Caribbean, particularly on the island of Montserrat, where Irish surnames such as O'Connor, Fitzgerald and O'Carroll are still to be found. Montserrat is the only country outside Ireland where St Patrick's Day is a public holiday. The date also commemorates a failed uprising by Afro-Caribbean slaves and members of the island's free black community on the same date in 1768. On entering Montserrat a shamrock is stamped on your passport and the crest of a woman dressed in green holding a cross and harp is included on the island's flag.

The walls that Cromwell would have had to breach in his attack had surrounded Drogheda since medieval times. They were completed in 1334, enclosing a large area on both sides of the river comparable in size to Dublin at that time, making Drogheda one of the largest fortified towns of the period. Not much of the wall survives today, but a portion of it can still be seen to the south of St Laurence's Gate, which stands at the top

St Laurence's Gate.

of St Laurence Street and is one of the most impressive sights in the town. The gate led to the friary of St Laurence, which was located just outside the town walls. St Laurence's Gate is a twin-towered barbican, which was a type of fortified structure used to defend the main gate to a town or castle. One of the finest examples of a barbican in Ireland, if not Europe, it was one of ten original entrances allowing access to the town. The two circular towers of the gate, each with four floors, are joined by an archway that has a groove for a portcullis. The lower part of the gate dates from the thirteenth century, while the upper third was added in the fifteenth century. This enormous barbican provided a clear view along the river estuary and would have supplied an early warning to the town of any seaborne invasion.

Also on St Laurence Street is Drogheda's Municipal Art Gallery, the Highlanes Gallery. It is housed in the former Franciscan friary and church, and contains Drogheda's important municipal art collection, which dates from the seventeenth century, as well as visiting exhibitions. Admission is free. The Franciscan friary church was constructed in 1829 around an earlier Franciscan foundation and was given to the town by the Franciscans in 2000.

Further down St Laurence Street, on the corner with Shop Street, is the Tholsel, originally the hall in which town taxes were paid. Public floggings and hangings took place in front of this building. The current building was erected in 1770 to replace an earlier wooden-framed tholsel, and this was the centre for the local government, Drogheda Corporation, until 1889. The building was then converted to a bank, a function it served until 2009. One of the oldest buildings in the town, the Tholsel has been home to the local tourist information office since 2010.

The tower surmounting the building houses a large four-faced clock.

The Tholsel.

Just up the hill from the Tholsel, off St Peter's Lane, is St Peter's Church of Ireland Church, among the finest Georgian church buildings in Ireland and completed in 1757 on the site of a previous church which dated back to the thirteenth century. During Cromwell's attack in 1649 some of the defenders took refuge in the wooden steeple of the earlier church and it is alleged that Cromwell ordered the steeple blown up. The church building is not open to the public, other than for services and events. However, it is still well worth a visit to see the cadaver tomb cover, which can be found set into the back wall of the northeastern corner of the churchyard, near a locked gateway. The tomb, that of Sir Edmund Goldyng and his wife, Elizabeth Fleming, dates to 1556 and depicts their decomposing bodies surrounded by shrouds. Edmund is depicted with his bowels spilling out and his hands crossed on his waist below them. Most of his arms and the central section of his legs are missing. Elizabeth's figure shows a body with clear signs of decay and her spine is visible through her ribcage, her abdomen empty. Her hands rest along her body and her face is more skull-like than that of her husband. The top of each shroud is twisted and tied with a knotted rope. Generally this type of tomb was

The tomb of Sir Edmund Goldyng and Elizabeth Fleming.

made when the person for whom it was intended was still alive, to remind them of what was waiting for them after their death and to make them think of their own mortality: 'This is how you will end up!' Very often worms, maggots, toads and frogs are shown feasting on the rotting flesh. There are a number of these cadaver tombs in this area dating from the fourteenth and fifteenth centuries, when, as a result of the mortality rate from plagues, people became obsessed with death and the transience of life.

Also within this churchyard, near the north wall of the church, is the white gravestone of John Duggan, a private in the 17th Lancers and a survivor of the Charge of the Light Brigade at Balaklava. He served as sexton of St Peter's Church for ten years. His gravestone bears the motto 'Death or Glory'.

East of St Peter's graveyard is The Alleys, a set of almshouses for clergymen's widows erected with funding from Archbishop Narcissus Marsh, who went on to found the first public library in Ireland near St Patrick's Cathedral, Dublin in 1707. There are four terraces of these houses and the house at the end of each alley has a bow window. The Gothic tracery above the doors is an original feature.

Not to be confused with the Protestant church of the same name, St Peter's Catholic Church, on West Street, the main street of Drogheda, is probably best known for being home to the shrine of St Oliver Plunkett. Drogheda was the residence of the Catholic archbishops of Armagh until 1835, and Plunkett was Archbishop of Armagh and Primate of Ireland from 1669 to 1681, when he was executed in London, the last Roman Catholic martyr to die in England. His head is preserved in the west transept of the church's side altar.

Born at Loughcrew, Oldcastle, Plunkett trained for the priesthood abroad and was ordained in 1654. He was responsible for opening a number of schools in Drogheda and also introducing the Jesuit order to his diocese. Arrested in Dublin in 1679, Plunkett was the last victim of 'The Popish Plot', a conspiracy theory fuelled by intense anti-Roman Catholic feeling, which imagined an extensive Catholic conspiracy to assassinate King Charles II. Plunkett was tried for high treason, once in Ireland and then again in London. The trial in Dundalk collapsed as the witnesses being brought against him were found to be untrustworthy. The second trial, in which some of these same witnesses also took part, is generally regarded as a serious miscarriage of justice. Although the charge was never proven, Plunkett was hung, drawn and quartered at Tyburn in London in 1681.

After his execution his head was thrown onto a prepared fire nearby, but it was rescued by his friends. Scorch marks from the fire may still be seen on the left cheek of the head. The head was brought to Rome and other places before ending up in the care of the Dominican nuns in the Siena Convent, Drogheda, around 1725. When Plunkett was beatified in 1920 by Pope Benedict XV, the head was transferred to St Peter's Church. The nuns were apparently 'very crestfallen' over the loss of their

The shrine of St Oliver Plunkett.

important relic. In 1975 Oliver was made a saint at a canonisation ceremony in Rome.

St Oliver's head now stands in an impressive new shrine constructed in 1995. The shrine also includes his left clavicle, left scapula, ninth and tenth rib and left hemi-pelvic bone, as well as sacrum relics of St Oliver donated by Downside Abbey, a Benedictine community in England, around the time of his canonisation. There is a wonderful painting of him in his robes above the relics, and a rather more horrible one showing him being dragged through the streets of London. In a glass cabinet nearby, the door of the condemned cell where the saint was imprisoned before his execution is also preserved.

The relic of the True Cross.

A relic of the True Cross is also on display in the church. The tiny sliver of the cross on which Jesus Christ was crucified was presented to St Peter's in 2009 by the Archbishop of Ghent. A letter of authenticity accompanies the relic. When visiting St Peter's please remember that it is a church and visitors are asked to maintain a respectful silence.

Once the belfry of an extensive Dominican friary, the fourteenth-century Magdalene Tower set above a Gothic arch is a landmark in the northern part of the town, as is the tall cream building of the Lourdes Hospital, with the large cross on the front wall, where all the babies for this region are born. The Dominican church, an Augustinian church and the remains of an Augustinian abbey are down by the river.

One of the quirkiest sights in Drogheda is the 'Fenian Ram' sculpture found at the gates of the Scholar's Townhouse on King Street. Unveiled in 2014, it is a model of one of the prototype submarines designed by John Philip Holland, who developed the first submarine to be commissioned by the US navy. The connection with Drogheda

The Magdalene Tower.

A model of the Fenian Ram.

comes from the fact that Holland had been a teacher at the Christian Brothers' School in Drogheda; the Scholar's Townhouse building was previously the Christian Brothers' monastery. Born in Clare, Holland joined the Christian Brothers in Cork and in 1865 took up the position of teacher of mathematics and music at the school in Drogheda. While there, he designed a submersible duck which could dive into a lake and return to walk on dry land. In 1873 Holland left the Christian Brothers due to ill health and moved to America. Once there, he worked with the Fenian movement to build a submarine that could be used against the British Royal Navy, hence the name. The actual 'Fenian Ram' was constructed at Delamater Iron Works in New York and launched in May 1881, but soon afterwards the Fenians and Holland severed ties and, rather ironically, Holland went on to work with the Royal Navy, who launched their own submarine based on his designs in 1901.

On the south side of the River Boyne, and set on a high hill that offers a magnificent view of the town and the surrounding countryside, Millmount fort is Drogheda's most strategic location. Tradition holds that the hill is the burial site of Amergin, who was regarded as the first great Celtic poet and the originator of the arts of song, poetry and music. It has been suggested that the mound may be a passage grave, dating back to the Neolithic Age, but no excavation has ever been done. Hugh de Lacy constructed a motte and bailey on Millmount in the 1170s, having been granted the kingdom of Meath from the Shannon to the sea by Henry II. A stone tower was later constructed and from 1381 there was a windmill on top of the mound – hence the name. This building formed part of the defences of the town during the siege of Drogheda. A complex of military buildings was later constructed around a courtyard at the base of the mound.

In 1808 the original fortifications were demolished and the complex was re-named Richmond Barracks when the Martello tower which still crowns the hill today was erected. Martello towers were erected all along the coast by the British to defend Irish soil against a possible Napoleonic invasion from France. However, this fort saw no real action until 1922, when it was shelled by Free State forces during the Civil War and considerably damaged. Restored by Drogheda Corporation, the buildings now house a museum established by the Old Drogheda Society in 1974. It hosts a range of exhibits, including guild and trade banners stretching back two centuries, an industrial exhibition, a geological collection, a recreated nineteenth-century kitchen, an archaeological display and a military room. One of the most interesting exhibits is a Boyne coracle, a round, basket-type boat made from oxhide on a framework of hazel wands which was used for salmon fishing on the River Boyne until the middle of the twentieth century. The hide of this particular coracle was the skin of a black polly bullock that won a prize at the Drogheda Fat Stock Show in 1943. Millmount Museum, which won an International Gulbenkian Museum Award, is open all year round and a small admission fee is charged.

Millmount, with the Martello tower on top of the motte.

Beaulieu House and church.

Just ten minutes downriver from Drogheda is Beaulieu House, sited on lands originally owned by the Plunkett family. The house and gardens are open to the public during the summer months and to groups and for events at other times. The four-acre gardens and the church with its cadaver tomb are well worth visiting, but be warned, the church grounds are only open on an occasional basis. The cadaver tombstone at Beaulieu House is the best-preserved stone of its type in the area. A snake winds its way in one ear of the corpse and out the other. The house, one of the first unfortified big houses in Ireland, was erected in the 1660s for Sir Henry Tichbourne and is still occupied by his descendants.

The Hill of Ward (Tlachtga).
Courtesy of Aubrey Martin

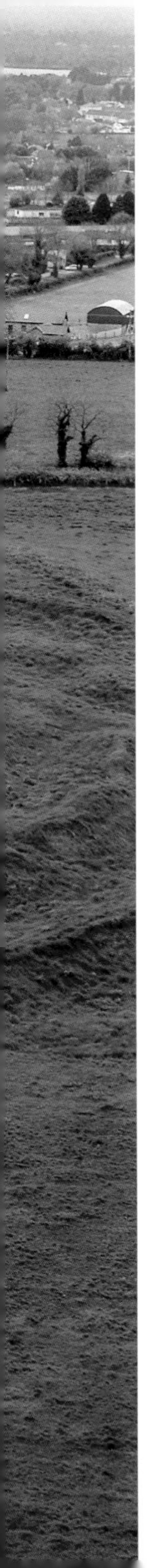

The Hill of *Ward*

Located southeast of the town of Athboy is the Hill of Ward, also called Tlachtga. A high status site associated with the high kings of Ireland and the kings of Munster, Tlachtga possibly originated in the Late Bronze or Early Iron Age as a ceremonial enclosure. It was one of the four royal Celtic hill-fort sites, along with Tara, Tailteann and Uisneach. The origin of these sites is explained in the legend of Tuathal. In the first century AD he arrived from Scotland to reclaim the throne of his father who had been deposed as high king. He fought twenty-five battles each against the forces of Ulster, Leinster and Connacht, and thirty-five against Munster. When he had conquered the whole country, Tuathal convened a conference at Tara, where he established laws and annexed territory around Tara from each of the four provinces to create the central province of Midhe for the high king. He is also said to have founded the four royal sites.

Tlachtga is a central raised enclosure surrounded by four banks and ditches that appear as a series of concentric earthworks on top of a small hill. The inner enclosure is approximately 50 metres in diameter. It is one of a very few recognised four-bank enclosures in Ireland, the others being Tara and Rathcroghan. The outer earthworks are approximately 150 metres in diameter. These earthworks have suffered much disturbance in their long history but are now a national monument. As with Tara, to get a real concept of the complex an aerial view is best. From the ground it is simply a field with banks, humps and hollows.

The Hill of Ward. *Courtesy of Aubrey Martin*

The name Tlachtga comes from a figure in Irish legend. She was a daughter of the druid Mogh Ruith, who was a student of Simon Magus, the alleged executioner of John the Baptist. Tlachtga fled from her father's house to give birth to three sons, Dorb, Cuma and Muacth, on the site named for her. She then died and was buried in the centre of Tlachtga. She is also said to have buried the *roth rámach* ('the oared wheel'), a magical flying machine built by her father and Simon Magus and powered by lightning, on the hill. In later stories this became an instrument of death, which struck dead any who saw, touched or heard it.

Samhain, the ancient Celtic festival we now call Halloween, is reputed to have originated on this site. Keating's seventeenth-century *History of Ireland* stated, 'It was there the Fire of Tlachtga was instituted, at which it was custom to assemble and bring together the druids of Ireland on the eve of Samhain to offer sacrifices to all the gods.' It was believed that a great fire was lit on the site on Samhain Eve, summoning all 'the priests, augurs and druids of Ireland to consume the sacrifices that were offered to their pagan gods'. It was decreed that all fires within the kingdom were to be extinguished and rekindled using the sacred flame of Tlachtga. The top of the hill was usually the preserve of the druids, and was only accessible to ordinary people on the great festival of Samhain. The tradition of Halloween bonfires continues throughout Ireland to this day.

The Samhain festival in Athboy near Tlachtga.

The great festival of the dead marked the coming of the long winter nights and the beginning of the Celtic New Year. The winter fires were ignited as the sun went down on the eve of Samhain. The Celts believed that this was a time of transition, when the veil between our world and the next came down, and the spirits of all who had died during the year moved on to the next life. This explains why the ghost is still an essential part of the mythology of modern Halloween. With the coming of Christianity the festival was incorporated into the Christian calendar as a time of remembrance for the holy souls, allowing the Samhain festival of the ancestors to retain its relevance. Irish immigrants carried the Halloween tradition to North America in the nineteenth century. Locally, a festival has been developed around the tradition of Halloween called 'The Spirits of Meath', which runs for most of October and into November.

It is thought that Tlachtga was also a place of pilgrimage for women who were childless. These women would bring their slaves' children to be sacrificed by the druids in the hope that the spirit of the sacrificed child would enter their bodies and be reborn.

Tlachtga has played a role in various historical events of significance. According to the *Annals of the Four Masters*, in 1022 the High King Máel Sechnaill defeated the Vikings at the Battle of Ath Buidhe Tlachtga at the foot of the hill. There was great slaughter that day and Máel Sechnaill won back a legendary collar of gold that had been stolen by the Vikings.

In 1166 Ruaidrí Ua Conchobair defeated his rival and became the undisputed high king of Ireland. Ua Conchobair sought to unite his people, so he summoned 'the power and the patriotism of the day' to a great convention at Tlachtga. The prelates and princes of the northern half of the country assembled on the hill. The *Annals of the Four Masters* record: 'They passed many good resolutions at this meeting, respecting veneration for churches and clerics, and control of tribes and territories, so that women used to traverse Ireland alone.'

In 1172 Tigernán Ua Ruairc, chief of Breifne, who had been granted east Meath by the high king and was not prepared to give this up to the invader Hugh de Lacy, arranged to meet his Anglo-Norman rival at Tlachtga. The two men were to come alone and unarmed to discuss the limits of their territories. Both went up the hill to negotiate, but only one came back down – Hugh de Lacy. One side asserted that Ua Ruairc produced a battle-axe from beneath his robe and attacked de Lacy, while the other side alleged that Ua Ruairc was treacherously killed and beheaded. Whatever happened, Ua Ruairc's headless body was sent to Dublin and gibbeted with the feet upwards on the northern side of the city, while his head was erected over the door of Dublin Castle.

During a recent archaeological survey a medieval settlement was discovered to the east of the hill, along with a possible cairn site. The geophysical survey also revealed the existence of a large enclosure running underneath the visible monument, showing that it predates the monument. Its ditch is approximately 3 metres in width, cut through the limestone bedrock. Constructed without the use of metal tools, it has been suggested that the ditch was excavated by fire setting. This involved lighting large fires on the rock and, when they reached peak temperature, cooling the rock suddenly with water, forcing the rock to split and splinter. The remains of a very young child were discovered carefully placed at the base of the ditch and covered with large flat stones. The infant was probably less than ten months old when he died, and the remains have been radiocarbon-dated to the fifth century AD.

Excavations on the Hill of Ward. *Courtesy of Joe Conlon*

When Cromwell arrived in Ireland in 1649, it is said that he camped on the Hill of Ward. One story claims that he had his cannon turned on Lord Robert Plunkett of Rathmore and his nine sons as they approached the Hill of Ward to discuss truce terms, killing them all in an instant. Lady Plunkett, who was watching from the tower of Rathmore Castle, saw what had happened and was so shocked that she fell to her death.

Tradition states that John Bligh received Rathmore Castle and estate from Cromwell on the Hill of Ward. It was believed that Bligh was granted all the land he could see from the top of the hill – Rathmore, Athboy, Ballivor and Kildalkey – 28,000 acres in all. His descendants held the lands until 1908.

Rathmore Church is a ruined medieval church just to the north of the Hill of Ward, on the Athboy to Navan road. It was constructed by the Plunkett family of Rathmore Castle, who were relatives of the Plunketts of Dunsany, Killeen and Loughcrew. Within the vestry is the effigy tomb of Sir Thomas Plunkett (d. 1471) and his wife Mary Anne Cruise. Sir Thomas is dressed in full armour, and a dog, a sign of fidelity, sleeps at his feet. The figure of Mary Anne is badly damaged, with few details remaining. This tomb originally stood in the church but was later moved to the sacristy to protect it from the elements. Inside the church ruins is a stone with a labyrinth engraved on it and outside is the shaft of a wayside cross.

In the fifteenth century Sir Christopher Cruise held the estate of Rathmore, together with Moydarragh and Cruicetown. He married late in life and this marriage resulted in a pregnancy and the possibility of a direct heir. His nephews, who had expected to inherit, were distressed at the news that they might be superseded, so they plotted to murder Sir Christopher and his wife as they walked along the avenue to Moydarragh Castle. When the attack began, Sir Christopher ordered his wife to run to the castle for reinforcements while he held off the ruffians with his sword, but when she returned her husband was dead.

Lady Cruise ordered that her husband be buried and, fearing for her own life, had a rumour spread that she was seriously ill. She gathered all the plate and treasures in the castle and had them sunk in the nearby lake. Then she had herself placed in a coffin as though dead and carried to Rathmore Castle. Once there she collected more treasure and used it to fill the coffin which was buried in her place, while she collected all the title deeds to Rathmore and Cruicetown and fled to London. There, she gave birth to a daughter named Mary Anne and they lived on the revenue from the treasures Lady Cruise had been able to bring from Ireland. When these funds ran out, the two had to make a living washing laundry on the banks of the River Thames. One day, while singing a song in Irish which her mother had composed listing all the lands which her family had held in Ireland, Mary Anne was heard by a young Irish lawyer, Sir Thomas Plunkett. He understood the words and went to meet the singer. Mary Anne impressed him so much that he accompanied her home, where her mother showed him the title deeds. Sir Thomas married Mary Anne and secured the return of her lands, so he won more than her heart when he married her! A cross commemorating the marriage was erected in the grounds of Killeen Castle, now a private golf club. The remains of the cross can be seen just off the avenue leading to the clubhouse.

Athboy, the nearest town to the Hill of Ward, was the birthplace of Frederick Harvey, who was awarded the Victoria Cross for single-handedly capturing a machine-gun post at Guyencourt during the First World War, and of Fr Eoghan Ó Gramhnaigh, a founding member of Conradh na Gaeilge (the Gaelic League) in 1893. His booklets, *Simple Lessons in Irish*, did much to promote the native language. A statue to Ó Gramhnaigh stands in the grounds of St James', the local Catholic church.

In 1935 an Irish-speaking area, the Gaeltacht of Ráth Chairn, was founded in an area just south of the hill, when twenty-seven families from Connemara were moved to Meath. Each family was provided with a house and a small farm. The resettlement aimed to address the poverty of the families on the western seaboard and to introduce the Irish language as a spoken language into an English-speaking area. There were later additions of further families from the west. As Irish speakers, the newcomers stood out from the local people and it took a while for them to be accepted by some locals. The Irish language and their common roots in Galway were the bonds that enabled the new community to survive. Today the Gaeltacht area has a thriving community, with a co-op, primary school, secondary school and church.

The statue of Fr Eoghan Ó Gramhnaigh.

St Colmcille's House.

Kells

For most people when Kells is mentioned the first thing that springs to mind is the *Book of Kells*, the beautifully illuminated manuscript now on display in the Old Library in Trinity College, Dublin. But there is much more to Kells than that. Founded in AD 806 by monks from St Colmcille's monastery on Iona in Scotland, this monastery was one of the great centres of Celtic Christianity. It was a major artistic centre in the early medieval period and the surviving remains include a wonderful collection of high crosses, an oratory and a round tower.

The name Kells derives from the Irish *Ceanannas Mór* or *Ceann Lios*, meaning great fort, so it has been suggested that there may once have been a royal residence on the site and that the curved streets of the town, Carrick Street, Castle Street and Cross Street, follow the line of its earthwork enclosure. There may also have been an inner enclosure constructed around the church. The name is also sometimes interpreted as 'head fort', which is reflected in the name of Headfort House and the hereditary title of the Marquess of Headfort, as well as some street names in Kells itself. Following Irish independence, many of the old Irish place names were reinstated. In 1929 *Ceanannas Mór* was made the town's official name and this survived until 1993, when the popularly used Kells was once more restored.

According to later tradition St Colmcille founded a monastery at Kells about AD 554, although there is no actual evidence for this. Despite this, his story is closely linked with that of Kells. Colmcille (meaning dove of the church), known in the Anglican Church as Columba, was originally from Donegal and founded monasteries throughout Ireland, including Derry, Swords, Raphoe and Durrow. Various stories exist to explain why the saint eventually left Ireland, but the most common one relates to a falling out with his teacher, St Finian. While studying at a monastery in Moville, Colmcille was reading a beautifully illuminated book of psalms belonging to Finian. When Colmcille was refused permission to copy the book, he did so secretly. But his actions were discovered and Finian asked King Diarmuid to decide who owned the copy. Diarmuid, making the first copyright decision in the world, decreed: 'To every cow its calf and to every book its copy.' Colmcille was dismayed at the outcome and a war broke out between his kinsmen and the high king's men. A large number of people were killed and Colmcille, blaming himself for the loss of life, decided his penance was to leave Ireland and never come back. He left for Scotland, where he founded a monastery on the island of Iona.

In 793 the monastery on Iona heard alarming news that the monastery at Lindisfarne in northeast England had been viciously attacked by raiders from across the sea. Two years later Iona itself was attacked and destroyed. The abbot and monks decided to move to Ireland for safety and established the monastery at Kells. However, in a few short years the Vikings had turned their attention to Ireland and Kells fell foul of their raids in 919, 950 and 969. Following each attack it was rebuilt.

As time went on the monastery faded in importance. It was

eventually replaced by an Augustinian monastery, founded in the mid-twelfth century, but the successor never achieved even a portion of the status of the original monastery.

In Anglo-Norman times a priory of the Hospitallers of Saint John of Jerusalem was established in Kells and the site of this monastery may also be visited, as it is now a graveyard, just off Headfort Place.

The Vikings were not the only outsiders to bring chaos to the settlement at Kells. In 1315 Edward Bruce, brother of Robert the Bruce, King of Scotland, burned the town of Kells to the ground. Edward aspired to the kingship of Ireland and his campaign also deflected English forces from the campaign against Scotland. The Bruce campaign in Ireland lasted for three years, during which there was unusually bad weather and disastrous harvests. Edward was defeated and killed at Faughart, outside Dundalk, in 1318, by an Anglo-Irish army led by Sir John de Bermingham.

Kells was on the main routes to the north and the west from Dublin and bordered the territory of the Irish clan of O'Reillys. Raids by the Irish into the English-controlled part of Ireland in the 1400s led to a drop in population in Kells as a result of the high taxation imposed on merchants to maintain the town walls. The town was devastated by the Confederate Wars of the 1640s and purchased in 1653 by Thomas Taylor, whose family was to dominate the area for the next 250 years. In 1760 the head of the family became Baron Headfort and ten years later Headfort House on the outskirts of the town was completed as the family residence. In the late eighteenth century the part of the town nearest Headfort estate was reconstructed as a Georgian estate village.

For the visitor to Kells today, the main place of interest is the site of the monastery. It was located on the highest point of the hill, where St Columba's Church of Ireland Church, constructed in 1778 by Thomas Taylor, first Earl of Bective, is located today. In the grounds of the church can be found the tenth-century round tower and four high crosses. There is still much discussion as to the purpose of this type of tower, but the most popular idea is that they were used as storehouses for the treasures of the monastery, a lookout spot and a place of refuge during attacks. It has also been suggested that they could have been a *cloigtheach* (bell tower). The grounds are usually open to the public and visitors are welcome to visit the graveyard; the church may also be open for visits.

The East or Unfinished Cross and round tower.

Kells' imposing round tower, unlike most other examples, has five windows at its top. Most round towers had four, one for north, south, east and west, but the five windows in the Kells tower allowed a watch to be kept on the five approach roads to the monastery. Access to the upper floors was by means of ladders, with each floor being illuminated by a single window. Today the doorway appears quite low, but that is because in the intervening years the ground level has been raised around the base of the tower by burials. The doorway faces east, in line with the west door of the associated church which no longer survives. The stonework around the door is different to the rest of the tower. It may date to after 1076, the year a claimant for the high kingship of Ireland took refuge in the tower but was forcibly removed and murdered. Local tradition says that any girl who rubs her skirt against the wall of the round tower will never leave Kells.

The four high crosses in the churchyard are dated to the ninth and tenth centuries. High or Celtic Crosses generally have a distinctive ring or circle around the head of the cross. While some say that this represents the old gods of the sun and the moon being superseded by the new Christian God of the cross, it could simply be a structural feature to add strength to the cross arms. The use of 'high' to describe these crosses may simply refer to their height, although not all high crosses are tall. This type of cross was decorated with scenes from the Bible on the base, shaft and arms. It could be said that they are really books in stone, and they may have been used to educate the illiterate about biblical stories. Some historians suggest that they were painted.

The closest of the high crosses to the round tower is the cross of St Patrick and St Columba, also known as the South Cross, which was erected in the ninth century. On the base is an inscription:

'PATRICII ET COLUMBE CR', a dedication to Saints Patrick and Columba. Carved from a single block of sandstone, the east face has scenes of Adam and Eve, and Cain killing Abel in the bottom panel; above that are the Three Children in the Furnace; and above that Daniel in the Lions' Den. On the right side of the head of the cross the raven brings bread to St Paul and St Anthony.

The Cross of St Patrick and St Columba.

The Broken Cross or West Cross stands at the west end of the graveyard, and only the shaft of the cross remains. The scenes that survive include the Baptism of Christ and, on the reverse, Adam and Eve and Noah's Ark. Christ's baptism takes place in the River Jordan, but the carver depicted two springs, clearly believing that there were two rivers, the Jor and the Dan!

In the graveyard on the north side of the church, the East Cross or Unfinished Cross provides an idea of how the great high crosses may have been carved. The panels have been blocked out for carving, but only the crucifixion scene on its east face has been partially completed. Carved on site, this cross was buried for a long period before being re-erected. Some speculate that the carver may have been killed in a Viking raid or driven far from Kells by a Viking attack, never to return.

The West Cross, also known as the Broken Cross.

Top: An image of the baptism of Christ from the West Cross. *Bottom*: An image of Adam and Eve from the West Cross.

All that remains of the North Cross, located by the bell tower, is the base. The only surviving portion of the medieval church, the tower, was rebuilt by Hugh Brady, Bishop of Meath, in 1578, as outlined in the inscription on it. A spire was added in 1783, shortly after the new church was completed.

Lying against the south wall of the current church is an early Christian sundial. This would originally have lain flat and a piece of metal would have been placed in the hole in the centre to allow the sun to cast its shadow. It marked the time for prayer for the monks during the day.

A detail of the sundial.

Situated on Church Lane, beyond and to the left of the north wall of St Columba's, is a stone oratory known as St Colmcille's House. Dating from the eleventh century, this small church building was strategically positioned at one of the highest points in the town. The building may have once housed relics of St Colmcille. The roof is barrel-vaulted, with three small chambers in the roof space, possibly sleeping quarters, reached by a long ladder. The largest chamber once held a large stone slab, 2 metres long and one-third of a metre thick, known as Colmcille's bed. In the 1830s a poor family who were living in the building were accused of sheep stealing. The discovery of sheep carcasses in the roof croft confirmed their guilt. In the 1980s the lock on the entrance to the oratory was broken and Colmcille's bed disappeared. The current entrance is modern and the present ground floor was the basement of the building; the original door was at the west end and about 2 metres off the ground. The building is generally kept locked but it is accessible to visitors: access arrangements are on display on the gate. Locals believe that a tunnel, constructed as far back as Viking times, existed from St Colmcille's House to St Columba's Church as an escape route.

Outside the Old Courthouse Heritage Centre stands what is probably Kells' most famous high cross, the Market Cross. It was originally a termon or boundary cross, meaning that any criminal who reached the cross was safe from pursuit. It used to stand in the commercial market, at the intersection of Cross Street and Market Street, and was high enough to be seen and used as a meeting point. Any deals done under the cross had to be honest deals, as they were carried out under a cross. In the centre of the head on the east side of the cross is a scene of Daniel in the Lions' Den. To the right of this is the Sacrifice of Isaac and to the left is the Temptation of St Anthony. The top panel of the shaft shows Adam and Eve, and Cain killing Abel. This scene features on many high crosses and seems to have been a popular subject. On the west face the centre of the cross shows the crucifixion. Non-religious subjects also feature on this cross, with a scene on the west face of the base depicting either a deer hunt or a man herding animals. Interestingly it also seems to show mythological subjects, with what appear to be

Above: The Market Cross.
Left: The hunt scene at base of the Market Cross.

centaurs on the north face of the base. This cross bears a later inscription: 'This cross was erected at the charge of Robert Balfe of Callierstown, being sovereign of the corporation of Kells, anno domini 1688'; a biblical panel on the shaft was removed to accommodate this. The cross was allegedly used as a gallows to hang rebels after the 1798 rebellion. Following an accident with a bus, the cross was moved from the town centre to a position of safety in front of the Old Courthouse.

Of course you can't talk about Kells without mentioning the *Book of Kells*, one of the most beautiful illuminated manuscripts of the western world, which has been described as 'The Work of Angels'. It has long been thought that the book was written in Iona and only finished in Kells, but the recent discovery of the Donore Hoard of decorated bronze artefacts at nearby Moyalty, which predate the book by a century but bear many of the designs displayed within it, has caused experts to re-examine this theory.

The book contains the four Gospels of the New Testament – Matthew, Mark, Luke and John – together with various charters, texts and tables. The type of script is known as insular majuscule. Created around AD 800, the *Book of Kells* was written on vellum made from about 185 calf skins. It is known that the monks in Kells kept a herd of as many as 1,200 cattle, which provided food and milk for the monastery. Rare and expensive dyes were used in the book, some imported from the Mediterranean and as far away as Afghanistan. A large, well-equipped scriptorium would have been required. At least three talented scribes were involved in the decoration. It seems the book was never finished, for reasons unknown, and some folios have also gone missing over time. It is believed that the book was made for display and ceremonial use, not to be read.

In 1007 the *Book of Kells* was stolen from Kells monastery. It was discovered two months and twenty days later 'under a sod' a few hundred metres away without its jewelled and gold cover and with some of its pages missing. Following the Dissolution of the Monasteries the book was kept by the retiring abbot and then passed into the hands of his family, the Plunketts. In 1653 it was sent to Dublin for safekeeping by Governor of Kells Charles Lambert. It then came into the possession of Archbishop James Ussher and was donated to Trinity College by his nephew, Henry Jones, in 1661 when he became Bishop of Meath. How the book came into his possession is unclear. The book, now bound in four volumes, is on permanent display at the college, where two of the volumes are usually displayed at a time, one showing a major illustration and the other showing typical text pages. Every few years a new campaign commences in Kells to have a section returned to the place it was named after, so far without success.

The monastery at Kells also had a strong metalwork tradition. The most famous example of this is the Kells Crozier, dating to around AD 1000. On the interior arch of its crook is an engraving 'OR DO CONDUILIG OCUS DO MELFINNEN', asking for prayers for Cúduilig and Maelfinnén. The historian, George Petrie, identified the names as belonging to ecclesiastical figures from Kells. It is now on display in the British Museum in London, having been discovered in 1850 behind a cupboard that had not been moved in the previous sixty years in a London solicitor's office. The crozier subsequently was the property of several owners, including Cardinal Wiseman, before being purchased by the museum in 1859. In 2000 a replica was made and is exhibited in Kells town hall, along with a facsimile of the *Book of Kells*.

Another example of Kells metalwork can be found in the National Museum of Ireland. The late eleventh-century shrine of the Cathach (Psalter) of St Columba was created by Sitric of Kells to the order of Cathbarr O'Donnell. *An Cathach*, possibly written by Colmcille, is a late sixth-century copy of the psalms and was an important relic used by Clan O'Donnell of Donegal as a rallying cry and protector in battle.

Kells is not only famous for its physical remains. Distinguished locals include Dick Farrelly, composer of 'The Isle of Innisfree', a hit for Bing Crosby and theme of the film *The Quiet Man*, which starred Maureen O'Hara, the town's most famous native. She is commemorated with a bust at Bective Place. Jim Connell from nearby Kilskyre wrote the socialist anthem 'The Red Flag' and is remembered each year on May Day in Kells and Crossakiel.

Just off the road to Oldcastle, north of the town, is St Colmcille's Well. A narrow walkway leads down to the well. In the early part of the twentieth century large crowds assembled there on the eve of St Colmcille's Day and recited the holy rosary in honour of the saint. Townspeople decorated the well with flowers and candles, and people visited it to pray and brought home water to drink. During the evening the local band played popular tunes. According to local tradition five fish appeared in the well every year on the eve of St Colmcille's Day. The annual pattern day (a date dedicated to a saint) is now celebrated on 9 June, the anniversary of Colmcille's death in AD 597.

On the western outskirts of Kells stands the spire or tower of Lloyd, the only inland lighthouse in Ireland. Twenty-five miles from the sea, the tower was erected in 1791 as a folly by the first Earl of Bective, supposedly to honour his father, the Marquess of Bective. Some believe the tower was built for the family to watch

The Tower of Lloyd.

horse racing and the hunt in comfort. Others say it was erected to provide employment at a time of economic hardship. It is possible to view five counties from the top. The tower was restored in 1997 by a mobile phone company and is now open to the public at designated times. Nearby is the site of a paupers' graveyard. The area round the tower has been developed as a community park, with a children's playground, picnic tables and a ring walk.

In the summer of 1868 John Abraham Ffolliott reputedly discovered a fairy coat as he went for a morning walk near a 'fairy ring' at Lloyd. The coat measured 16 centimetres from collar to hem, fully lined with a velvet collar and made of brownish-grey material in a style from the late eighteenth century.

To the southeast of Kells on the Navan road is Tailteann, the site of games held by the high kings of Ireland, which local lore claims were the template for the Olympic Games. Earthworks are scattered over the landscape, some visible and accessible, others not. The Tailteann Games were revived by the new Irish state in 1924 and were held again in 1928 and 1932. Celtic fairs held at Tailteann from the Iron Age up to the twelfth century AD were occasions for trial marriages. A tall wall was constructed with a number of small holes. Girls put their finger through the holes to be admired by the males on the other side. If a man liked a finger he selected its owner as a partner. The couple were married for a year and a day and would then return to Tailteann to either make it permanent or go back to the wall.

Finally, if you get the chance, there is a wonderful bog walk at Girley. Located 7 kilometres from Kells on the Mullingar road, there are two trails, a shorter of 1.5 kilometres and a longer of 6 kilometres, which cover a variety of forest and bogland and play host to a variety of bird life, plants and animals.

Cairn T, Loughcrew.
Courtesy of John Scarry

Loughcrew

About thirty passage tombs are spread across the Loughcrew hills in northwest Meath. The name is derived from the Irish *Loch Craobh*, meaning the lake of the branches, the name of the lake at the base of the ridge on which the cairns were constructed. Dating to before 3000 BC, this is one of the four main passage grave complexes in the country and is contemporary to or a little older than Newgrange.

Although commonly referred to as tombs, these cairns were so much more. They were ritual monuments, places where gatherings took place. The sites are infused with a sense of power, superstition and mysticism. Constructed by a community of Neolithic farmers, their location on the highest point of the county is striking. The complex is laid out across three hilltops: Carnbane East, Carnbane West and Patrickstown. There are thirteen cairns on Carnbane West and seven on Carnbane East, with the centrepiece on the latter hill being Cairn T. The large stones of the cairns abound with megalithic art: lozenges, circles, dots, chevrons, zigzags, triangles and leaf shapes. The third hill is Patrick's Hill in Patrickstown, where there are the remains of four cairns, three stone circles and a medieval motte.

It was common that a site like this would overlook settlements. The surrounding area is relatively flat and there are fabulous views to the east and south across the plains of Meath and to the lakelands of Cavan to the north. On a clear day it is possible to make out eighteen of Ireland's thirty-two counties, and the hills of Tara and Slane can be picked out on the eastern horizon.

It is amazing that the mapmakers of the Ordnance Survey completing the first scientific mapping of the country in the 1830s did not record these monuments, although their existence was recognised in local folklore. The area of Loughcrew was traditionally known in Irish as *Sliabh na Cailleach,* meaning the hill of the witch or hag. Jonathan Swift recorded how local folklore described the witch filling her apron with stones with which she would build her tomb. The cairns were formed when these stones fell out of her apron onto the summits of the three hills. Local folklore also claims that the witch plummeted to her death before she reached the final hill. A mound on Patrickstown hill supposedly marks her burial site. In older times the witch or hag was not the feared creation we dread in the present day – she was a respected, wise old woman who had gained special knowledge of the natural world and could use it to cure minor ailments and illnesses.

The cairns were rediscovered by a schools inspector, Eugene A. Conwell, while on a picnic with his wife in 1863. It was he who undertook the first thorough exploration and mapping of the tombs, allocating a letter from the alphabet to each tomb. Conwell suggested that the main cairn, Cairn T, was the tomb of Ollamh Fodhla, the ancient lawgiver and king of Ireland, but further research would determine that the tombs were constructed over 2,000 years before this legendary figure was meant to have lived. Conwell hoped that a stone like the Rosetta

A decorated orthostat from Cairn T. *Courtesy of John Scarry*

stone would be discovered to illuminate the meaning of the artwork, but alas, this was not to be.

Cairn T dominates the crest of Carnbane East. The mound is 35 metres in diameter, with a 5-metre passage ending in a cruciform chamber. The largest of its thirty-seven large kerbstones, the Hag's Chair, is a massive block with imposing armrests carved from the stone and facing north. A deeply incised cross carved into its seat was noted by Conwell as a mapmaking mark, although others have claimed that the stone was used as a mass rock during penal times. It may also have served as an altar in pagan times, as it provides an unobscured view of the two neighbouring hills with their tombs to the east and west. Local lore states that a modern visitor seated on the chair will be granted a single wish.

Cairn T from the air.
Courtesy of Aubrey Martin

Inside Cairn T was constructed a cruciform chamber with a corbelled roof and some of the most beautiful examples of Neolithic art in Ireland. The builders used local limestone for the structure of the cairn and sandstone for the decorated stones. A high sill stone has to be stepped over at the end of the passage to enter the central chamber. The capstone of the chamber is missing and a modern vent shaft allows in light and air. When Conwell first excavated the tomb in 1864 he discovered 'a hatful' of cremated remains under a stone at the centre of the chamber. A quartz wall was discovered behind the kerbstones. The quartz may have come from the Wicklow mountains. The name of the townland, Carnbane, is translated as white mound, which could suggest that quartz was used on the outside of the cairn.

The passageway is aligned with the rising sun of the spring and autumn equinoxes and on these days people gather at dawn in the cairn to watch the sunlight enter the chamber and illuminate the inside of the tomb. This occurs when the day and night are of equal length, around 20/21 March and 22/23 September and a few days on either side. The sunlight moves from left to right on the back stone, highlighting the carved symbols for about sixty minutes. The cairns are opened on three mornings by OPW staff. If you want to attend, dress warmly and arrive early (the guides are there from 6 a.m. at the spring equinox and from 7.15 at the autumn equinox) as there are usually large crowds. There is no pre-booking of places and the guides will try to accommodate as many as possible.

Around Cairn T are a number of smaller satellite tombs which have been scavenged for stone, although many have the stones of the tombs intact, some with decoration. Further damage was caused by the excavations carried out by Conwell, as he was not an archaeologist and partly destroyed some of the tombs.

One of the cairns excavated by Conwell on Carnbane West, Cairn H, was re-excavated by Joseph Raftery in 1943. He discovered some 3,000 bone fragments at foundation level, 300 of which were carved with designs characteristic of the Celtic Iron Age *La Tène* style. This evidence suggests that the cairns had continuity of use from the Stone Age to the Iron Age.

The decorated back stone from cell 6 in Cairn L, next to Cairn H, Carnbane West. *Courtesy of John Scarry*

There is a small car park below Carnbane East and from it there is a pathway up the hill. Access to the hill and monuments is free. It is not a long walk but the ground is uneven and steep, and there is no wheelchair access. There are benches set beside the route so you can take a rest. During the summer months Cairn T is open to the public and there is a guide who will provide free information and a torch if requested. During the rest of the year Cairn T is locked but the key can be obtained at the nearby Loughcrew Gardens. A deposit against the return of the key is usually requested. Bring a torch to see the extraordinary artwork. Photography is allowed within the tomb.

Loughcrew Megalithic Centre is located a short distance from the car park in the traditionally styled home of Maggie Heaney. A tour will bring you back to a simpler time in Irish life. There is also a cosy café, a craft shop, a cottage hostel, a tranquil caravan park and a yurt. Guided tours are also provided to the cairns from the centre.

Carnbane West is private property and permission from the landowner is required for access. Please note the approach roads are very narrow and extreme caution is needed. There are also no toilet facilities. On the R154 approach road to Oldcastle there is a viewing point at Patrickstown from where you can see the plains of Meath and the lakes of Cavan.

The estate of Loughcrew was the seat of a branch of the Plunkett family, of which the martyred St Oliver is the most famous member. His feast day is 1 July and so an annual celebration in his honour is held each year at the ruins of Loughcrew Church in the gardens of the estate, on the first Sunday of July at 3 p.m. Loughcrew Gardens are generally open to the public from March to October every year. The ancient yew walk, medieval motte and St Oliver Plunkett family church ruins may be visited.

North of the Loughcrew cairns is Oldcastle, an eighteenth-century estate town laid out by the local landlords, the Naper family, who were granted lands confiscated from the Plunkett family. The market house at the centre of the square is now a commercial enterprise. Oldcastle Workhouse, now demolished, was an internment camp for German and Austrian natives during the First World War. In 1902 a newspaper entitled *Sinn Féin* was first published in Oldcastle, the first prominent use of the words.

About fifteen minutes by car to the northwest of Oldcastle along the R154 is Mullaghmeen Forest, the largest beech forest in Ireland. It also has Sitka spruce, Scots pine and noble fir, along with an interesting collection of native trees. Various looped walks are laid out through the forest.

Further south is Fore Abbey, which was founded as an early Christian monastery by St Féichín and succeeded by a Benedictine foundation in the twelfth century. Because of its relationship with its French motherhouse, Fore was regularly seized by the English authorities as 'alien property' when England was at war with France. Located in a picturesque valley, Fore is well known for the Seven Wonders of Fore: the anchorite in a stone, the water that will not boil, the monastery built on a bog, the mill without a millstream, the water that flows uphill, the tree which will not burn and the stone lintel raised by the saint's prayers. It is well worth a visit, and do examine the *columbarium* (dovecote) where the monks raised pigeons to eat.

The abbey gatehouse.

Mellifont

Founded in 1142 by St Malachy of Armagh, Mellifont was the first Cistercian monastery in Ireland. This significant event marked the re-organisation of the Irish Church and monastic system, bringing it into line with continental Europe. The Church in Europe had bishops, dioceses and parishes, while in Ireland it was loosely based around monasteries and tribal territories. Moreover, the Irish monasteries did not follow a recognised rule for behaviour and ritual. The Cistercians brought the first European-wide rule for monks to Ireland.

The name Mellifont is derived from the Latin *Font Mellis,* which means 'fountain of honey'. The monastery is located in a quiet river valley between Slane and Drogheda, well beyond the temptations of the world. The site is sometimes called Old Mellifont to distinguish it from New Mellifont in nearby Collon, where Cistercians from Mount Melleray in Waterford re-established a monastery in the 1930s on lands which had been part of the property of the original abbey.

St Malachy is best remembered for his prophecies relating to the papacy, although the authenticity of these has been called into question as they were not published until 1595, nearly 500 years after the saint died. It is said that when Malachy visited Rome in 1139 he had a strange vision about the future that foretold the identity of every pope, 112 in all, from his time until the end of time. Each pope is foretold in a short phrase. Pope John XXIII was described by Malachy as *Pastor et Nautas*, meaning pastor and sailor. Pope John was both a profoundly pastoral pontiff and had been patriarch of Venice. The prophecy described Pope Benedict as *Gloria Olivae*, which means the glory of the olive. The Benedictine order of monks have an affinity to the olive and one of their branches is named the Olivetan. According to the prophecy Pope Francis is the last pope. The prophecy is: 'in the final persecution of the Holy Roman Church there will reign Peter the Roman, who will feed his flock amid many tribulations, after which the seven-hilled city will be destroyed and the dreadful Judge will judge the people. The End.' Francis chose his papal name from Saint Francis of Assisi, whose full name was Francesco di Pietro di Bernardone – Pietro meaning Peter. Pope Francis also served on the Curia in Rome.

Malachy, as Archbishop of Armagh, led the reform of the Irish Church, supporting the introduction of dioceses and recognised orders of monks. While travelling to Rome, he lodged at the monastery at Clairvaux in France, where he became friendly with Abbot Bernard. Impressed by the Cistercian rule and discipline, on his return to Ireland Malachy dispatched a number of Irish novices to be trained under Bernard's direction.

The lands for the new monastery at Mellifont were gifted by the local king, Donnchad Ua Cerbaill. A mixed group of French and Irish monks formed the first community. The original church was constructed in the 1150s under the guidance of a French monk called Robert. However, the French monks quarrelled with the Irish monks and soon returned to Clairvaux, provoking Bernard to complain to Malachy. Bernard viewed the Irish at this time as being in the 'depth of barbarism ... never had he found men so shameful in their morals, so wild in their rites, so impious in their faith, so barbarous in their laws, so stubborn in discipline, so unclean in their life. They were Christians in name, in fact they were pagans.'

The church was consecrated in 1157 and High King Muirchertach Mac Lochlainn, who was in attendance, donated sixty ounces of gold and land near Drogheda to the new monastery. Dervorgilla, wife of Tigernán Ua Ruairc, the ruler of Breifne, also attended and presented sixty ounces of gold, a gold chalice for the altar of Mary and nine cloths for the other altars of the church. In 1152 Dervorgilla had been taken by Diarmait Mac Murchada, king of Leinster, although it is not clear if this was an elopement or an abduction. Some years later, in 1166, Mac Murchada was expelled from Ireland by High King Ruaidrí Ua Conchobair, who was allied to Ua Ruairc, and some sources attribute this action at least in part to Ua Ruairc's desire for revenge, despite the fact that Dervorgilla had been returned to him. Mac Murchada travelled to England, then France, where he offered fealty to King Henry II in return for support in retaking his kingdom. This resulted in the arrival of the Normans in Ireland and the connections and complications which have arisen from this link to England over the last 850 years. Dervorgilla is often painted as the scarlet woman whose elopement with Mac Murchada was the reason the English came to Ireland. She later entered the monastery at Mellifont, spending the last years of her life there and dying on 25 January 1193, aged eighty-five.

By 1170 Mellifont's congregation had grown to 100 monks and 300 lay brothers. From this initial Cistercian monastery more than thirty daughter houses were established, the first

Mellifont Abbey from the air.
Courtesy of Aubrey Martin

being Bective. However, by 1216 there had been a general breakdown of discipline and the abbot and monks refused to obey the rules of the General Chapter of the Cistercians – the governing body of the order. The Chapter appointed visitors from other monasteries to reform Mellifont, but in 1217 the abbot refused them admission and barred the abbey gate. This event became notorious as the 'Conspiracy of Mellifont'. Around 1220 a French abbot was appointed as abbot of Mellifont but he resigned after a short period when he discovered that his monks were plotting to kill him.

Contrary to Cistercian rules, there were women in the monastery. By 1228 a house of nuns had been established adjoining Mellifont and, even more scandalously, the abbot's house was situated next to the courtyard of the nuns' house. That year Stephen of Lexington, abbot of Stanley in England, arrived to solve the crisis. He appointed a new abbot, limited the number of monks and lay brothers, and ensured that those who entered could confess in French or Latin. This last condition was obviously an attempt to limit the number of troublesome Irish who could become monks. He also ordered the selling of the nuns' house.

Mellifont Abbey became one of the wealthiest abbeys in Ireland, with vast holdings of land. Despite this wealth, the monks of Mellifont lived simply and austerely, embracing the order's rules of silence, prayer, manual labour and seclusion from the world. There were two categories of monks: lay and choral. Many lay brothers were illiterate peasants who performed domestic or agricultural work for the community. They were bound by vows of chastity and obedience to their abbot but were allowed to follow a less demanding form of Cistercian life. The lay brothers wore a brown tunic instead of the white worn by the choral monks. For the choral monks daily life was divided between work, worship, reading and rest. Mass had to be said daily by each monk, so there were ten altars to facilitate this.

In 1488 Mellifont's abbot, Thomas Hervey, received a royal pardon for his support of the Lambert Simnel rebellion. The Yorkist faction had attempted to place the ten-year-old Simnel, whom they crowned Edward VI in Christchurch Cathedral in Dublin in 1487, on the throne of England. Supported by the Fitzgeralds of Kildare and Flemish mercenaries, Simnel's army invaded England but was defeated. King Henry VII of England pardoned Simnel, realising he was simply the pawn of older men, and provided him with a job cleaning pots in the royal kitchen.

During Henry VIII's Reformation, Mellifont was dissolved and the property came into the possession of the Moore family. Initially the Moores expanded the gatehouse and adapted it into a defensive tower house. Then they converted part of the monastery into a fortified manor house. The Chapter House remained in use and became a banqueting hall for the family, but the rest of the old religious buildings were destroyed.

In 1603 Mellifont was the site of the surrender of Hugh O'Neill, following defeat at the Battle of Kinsale, which ended the Nine Year War between the Gaelic chieftains and English forces. Baron Mountjoy, who was leading the English army, was aware of Queen Elizabeth's recent death and was anxious to conclude an agreement before the news became known to the Irish leaders, in case they fought on to secure better terms from the new king. The Treaty of Mellifont granted O'Neill much of what he had asked for, but the continuing distrust between

The Lavabo, Mellifont Abbey. © *Shutterstock*

the two sides led to the collapse of the Gaelic nobility with the Flight of the Earls in 1607; the Plantation of Ulster began shortly afterwards.

In 1661 the head of the family at Mellifont, Henry Moore, was created Earl of Drogheda. Henry came into possession of lands in what is now the centre of Dublin and developed a number of streets which bear his name and title: Henry Street, Moore Street, Earl Street and Drogheda Street. A small lane linking Moore Street to Henry Street was called Of or Off Lane. Drogheda Street was later renamed Sackville Street and is now O'Connell Street.

In 1690 the manor house played host to William of Orange, who used the Chapter House to hold his pre-battle conference prior to the Battle of the Boyne. The Moore family remained in possession of Mellifont until 1727, when the property passed to the Balfour family of nearby Townley Hall. A local story records that about 1755 the then owner gambled the blue marble doorway of the Chapter House in a game of cards. When he lost, the winner had it transferred to his residence where it was converted for use as a fireplace. The location of the original is not known, but a replica of the doorway can be found in St Patrick's Cathedral, New York, where it stands in the chapel of St Bernard and St Bridget.

By the early nineteenth century the Chapter House had become a pigsty. The monastery's walls were removed for building stone and the manor house suffered a similar fate. Much of the material was used to construct a mill on the nearby stream. Rubble and earth covered the foundations of the buildings. Excavations in the 1880s uncovered the foundations and outline of the buildings.

Most of the remains of the monastery today are simply foundations, although the entrance gateway, Lavabo and the Chapter House are all still partially standing. Mellifont was the first of the monasteries in Ireland laid out around a cloister and its plan was followed by many of the monasteries constructed in medieval times in Ireland. The church, on the north side of the cloister, was a large aisled building on a cruciform plan with side chapels. The Chapter House and day rooms for the choir monks, above which was the monk's dormitory, lay to the east of the cloister. To the south was the calefactory or warming room where the old and infirm monks went to get warm as there generally was only one other fire in the abbey, in the abbot's quarters. Next to this was the kitchen and the refectory where the monks ate their meals in a communal setting. On the west were storerooms and accommodation for the lay brothers. Finally, on the south side of the quadrangle, surrounded by the cloister, stood the Lavabo.

The Chapter House is the only roofed building surviving. Within this building there are some of the original tiles used for flooring. This was where the senior monks met in assembly on a regular basis, the meeting commencing with a chapter of the rule of the Cistercian order. In front of the Chapter House was the Abbot's Parlour where free talk, or *parlay*, was allowed at certain times.

The most unusual feature of the monastery is the octagonal Lavabo, dating to about 1200. A fountain of water issued in jets from a central column and fell into a basin in which the monks washed their hands before entering the refectory for their meals. Both their sins and grime were washed away. The Lavabo survived as the porch for the entrance hall to the Moore mansion. A small section of the cloister has been re-erected next to it.

On a hillside overlooking the abbey sit the remains of a small parish church and graveyard, access to which is behind the visitor centre. This church probably dates to the post-Reformation period but may have been on the site of an earlier church which the monks used for the local parishioners.

This quiet river valley is an ideal place for a picnic and access to the site is free. The small visitor centre operates during the summer, displaying fragments of sculptured stones and a model of the abbey. Guided tours are available on request for which there is a charge. The visitor centre is fully accessible for visitors with disabilities and a good part of the site is wheelchair accessible. The picnic tables are also wheelchair friendly.

The West Cross, north church and round tower at Monasterboice.

Monasterboice

Just north of Drogheda, Monasterboice is one of the oldest and most prestigious religious sites in all of Ireland. The site of an early monastery founded in the late fifth century by St Buite, what survives today is the cemetery, which incorporates two ruined churches, a round tower and the remains of three high crosses. The presence of such beautifully decorated high crosses, as well as the round tower, suggest that the monastery must have been a wealthy establishment, which would originally have covered a much larger area, spreading out into the neighbouring fields. Traces of a larger enclosure have been identified in the field to the south.

The name is derived from *Mainistir Bhuithe*, meaning the monastery of Buite. Very little is known about St Buite himself. It is said he trained in Wales and returned to Ireland via Scotland, where he brought the king of the Picts back to life. Another story relates how, at Monasterboice, St Buite was informed that the high king at Tara was about to behead a prisoner. He decided to appeal to the king for clemency. On his journey he found the River Boyne in flood, hampering his attempt to reach Tara. Holding out his staff, Buite struck the water and the waters parted like the Red Sea did for Moses. When Buite arrived at Tara the beheading had already taken place, but Buite was not to be defeated and he stuck the head back on the body and the man came back to life. However, in the rush to reattach the head, Buite put it on the wrong way round! The man spent the rest of his life as a gardener in Monasterboice.

Buite grew to be an old man and died in an unusual way. Walking one day in the monastery cemetery, he was filled with a desire for death and is said to have ascended a ladder provided by angels. The *Annals of the Four Masters* record AD 521 as the year of his death. In a final story of his life, Buite later returned to earth in a glass wheel to prophesy the birth of Colmcille, who was alleged to have visited the site on a later date. A disc of glass obscured Buite's face and enabled him to see without being seen, as viewing an inhabitant of Heaven would have been too much for ordinary mortals.

Not much is known about the history of the monastic settlement at Monasterboice. What is known is that in some cases abbacies became secular and administrative, with the abbot taking on a role more like a local lord and responsibility for the religious observance passing to another monk. Often succession of the office of abbot was passed down in families, not only from father to son but also to brothers and nephews. Monasterboice appears to have been one of these cases. When Abbot Corman of Monasterboice died in 764, he was succeeded by his son Dub-da-inber. At this time the rule of celibacy was not enforced in the Irish Church.

In 968, according to the *Annals of the Four Masters*, High King Domhnall Ua Néill plundered Monasterboice against 'the Foreigners' (Vikings) and burned 300 of them in one house. The Vikings had a settlement at Annagassan on the coast nearby and some of them had obviously taken to living in the vicinity of the monastery as it was the nearest major commercial centre. It is a common misconception that only Vikings raided the monasteries and destroyed them. Just as often a jealous Irish tribe which had a competing monastery would raid the opposition. For instance, the monastery at Clonmacnoise on the River Shannon was raided forty-six times between AD 700 and 1200; the Vikings

The western face of Muiredach's Cross, Monasterboice.
© *Shutterstock*

came thirteen times, while the native Irish ransacked the site on twenty-seven occasions and the Normans perpetrated six raids.

The last recorded abbot of Monasterboice died in 1122 and the monastery appears to have gone into decline following the foundation of nearby Mellifont in 1142.

Today, the remaining high crosses are the biggest draw to the site. On entering the graveyard, the first cross you will come across is Muiredach's Cross, or the South Cross, regarded as the finest high cross in the whole of Ireland. The shaft and arms are carved from a single block of sandstone. Named for Abbot Muiredach Mac Domhnaill, who died in 923, the inscription on the base reads *Or Do Muiredach Lasernad in Chros,* mean-

A scene depicting the arrest of Christ on Muiredach's Cross.

ing 'A prayer for Muiredach for whom the cross was made'. The cross stands 5.5 metres tall and is decorated on all sides with biblical images from both the Old and New Testaments, as well as snakes, beasts, spirals and other designs. It is not possible to decipher satisfactorily the meaning of all the panels, but the bottom panel of the western face depicts the arrest or mocking of Christ. In it the Roman soldiers wear the dress of Viking warriors from the tenth century and sport elaborate moustaches. Above that appears to be Doubting Thomas with his finger in Christ's wound. In the centre of the cross is a scene of the crucifixion. On the eastern face the centre of the cross depicts the Last Judgement, with the saved led by David with a harp on Christ's right and the damned on his left. All the good souls face Christ. The

A scene depicting the Last Judgement on Muiredach's Cross.

A scene depicting Adam and Eve, and Cain killing Abel on Muiredach's Cross.

Archangel Michael is weighing the souls, with the scales being tipped by a devil underneath. A devil with a trident pushes the bad souls, who have turned away from Christ, to eternal damnation. The four panels on the shaft show, from the top down, the adoration of the Magi, Moses striking water from the rock, David smiting Goliath and, in the bottom panel, Adam and Eve, and Cain killing Abel. The carver had some fun as well, carving two cats fighting at the base of the shaft, each with the other's tail in their mouths, and on the other side two Irish wrestlers each pulling the other's beards and two cats with kittens in their paws. The cross is capped with a stone replica of a gabled-roof church similar to the early Christian churches in Ireland.

Beyond Muiredach's Cross is the south church, the older of the two on site, dating to no later than the thirteenth century. It still has the remains of the chancel arch. In the northeastern corner of the south church there is a bullaun stone with a single depression, possibly a container for holy water. These are also called cursing stones or curing stones. Local folklore often attaches religious or magical significance to them, such as the belief that the rainwater collected in the stone's hollow has healing properties – these beliefs may pre-date Christianity.

Near the south church is the Gartland gravestone, erected in 1799, with an inscription in Irish, Latin and English. This is notable because the use of Irish on a stone at this time was very unusual. At the top of this tombstone is a depiction of the dead rising on the day of judgement.

Unusually, the north church, situated beside the round tower and dating to the fifteenth century, has no trace of a chancel, a normal part of church architecture. The partial remains of an early Christian cross slab lean against its south wall. An early Christian grave slab which lies on the ground surrounded by a railing near the north wall of the church is inscribed *Or Do Ruarcan*, meaning 'a prayer for Ruarcan'. Decorated with a cross, it can be difficult to spot amongst the later gravestones.

Right beside the side doorway to the north church is the West Cross. Standing at a height of 6.5 metres, it is the tallest high cross in Ireland. This cross was constructed of three pieces and is so weatherworn that it is difficult to distinguish the scenes in the panels. As with Muiredach's Cross, the West Cross was decorated on all four sides and topped with a replica of a gable-roofed church.

Built in the tenth century, the round tower at Monasterboice is the second highest in Ireland, the highest one being on Scattery

Island in the Shannon. It was divided into four storeys inside, connected with ladders. The top of the tower has been shattered by lightning and so is missing its conical cap. The tower served as a landmark on the great north–south road from Tara, which passed the monastery. Travellers on the road could take their rest in Monasterboice. The tower emphasised the importance of the monastery: a monastery with a round tower was more important than one with no round tower.

The tower at Monasterboice was burned in 1097, destroying the monastic library and other treasures stored there. This type of tower, with their wooden floors and ladders, would have made a good chimney if an invader got the opportunity to light a big enough fire. In 1871 the floors were restored, but the tower is closed to the public. Today the doorway is not far above ground level, as in the intervening years the ground level of the cemetery has been raised by burials.

Just to the right of the stairs leading to the door of the round tower is an interesting gravestone. It commemorates Mary, the wife of Nicholas Curran of Cotlerstown, who died in 1847, and also records the death of Nicholas and their three children three years later in New Orleans. Fleeing the Great Famine in Ireland, the family fell victim to yellow fever in Louisiana.

The third high cross, the simpler North Cross, can be found fenced off in the northeastern corner of the graveyard. The shaft has been reconstructed with a modern piece of stone. On its east face there is a lovely medallion composed of bosses and swirls. Also in this enclosure is a sundial marking the hours of prayer: 9 a.m., 12 noon and 3 p.m.

The Monasterboice graveyard is one of the longest continuously used burial grounds in the world. While the older gravestones mostly face east, as this is where Christianity says the Lord will appear on day of judgement, some of the newer gravestones face west, as do those of the parish priests. For the priests, this is because even in death they face their flock and keep a wary eye on them. Rev. James Campbell, Fr Henry McKee and Canon Patrick McCulla are among those keeping watch in Monasterboice. For the newer graves it is simply a matter of space.

Monasterboice is located in secluded countryside 8 kilometres northwest of Drogheda, just west of the M1. The graveyard is always open and access is free. There are toilet facilities and a car park across the lane from the monastic complex, as well as a voluntary guide service which operates at designated times.

Nearby, on the side of the old Dublin to Belfast road, is the papal cross commemorating the visit of Pope John Paul II in 1979. The papal visit occurred at a time of enormous violence in Northern Ireland and while the pope wanted to visit the North, security considerations overruled his wishes. Instead he came to Killineer, County Louth, which is in the Diocese of Armagh, part of which is in the South and part of which is in the North. On 29 September 300,000 pilgrims gathered there to hear him appeal to the men and women of violence: 'On my knees I beg you to turn away from the paths of violence and return to the ways of peace.' Nearly twenty years later an agreement was signed which finished the terror.

Donaghmore
round tower.

Navan

Navan spells the same forwards and backwards and so is a palindrome. The name may be derived from the Irish *An Uaimh*, meaning a cave or souterrain, and may be referring to a mound, possibly a Neolithic passage grave on the outskirts of the town. Alternatively, it may be derived from the name of a Celtic queen who, according to legend, was abandoned by her husband in Spain, travelled to Ireland in the hope of being reunited and died of a broken heart in Navan.

On Market Square, which is in fact a triangle, stands a sculpture of a bull being restrained by two men, recalling Navan's previous importance as a cattle-dealing town. The body is sculpted out of limestone and the plinth is of black granite. It was finished in 2003 but not installed until 2011 as there was some controversy over the cost of the project as well as the choice of subject.

Metge's Lane, just off the square, is named after a local landed family. Probably the most interesting member of this family was Lillian Metge. Following the death of her husband, Robert, Lillian returned to her hometown of Lisburn, where she threw herself into the suffragette movement. On the night of 31 July 1914 a huge explosion was heard all over the town. Panicked police officers discovered that a bomb had gone off in the cathedral. Glass and masonry

The Navan Bull.

were strewn around, as were a large number of suffragette flyers. Muddy footprints led the officers to Lillian's home. A local store owner told them that Lillian had recently purchased dynamite. There was a clear culprit and an angry crowd gathered as she was brought to jail. A week later she was released under bail of £100. However, due to the outbreak of the First World War no charges were pursued, as the authorities did not wish to upset the womenfolk whose support would be necessary for the war effort.

The Metge's Lane sign.

One of the first Catholic secondary schools in the country, St Finian's College, was established in Navan in 1802. The building still stands at the back of Academy Street but is in poor condition. The school's assembly hall had rounded rather than square ends and was named Power's Duck Egg after one of the headmasters. The school's most distinguished pupil was Fr Nicholas Callan, who invented the first induction coil in 1836 while a professor at Maynooth College. An induction coil produces a high voltage output from a low direct voltage input and is still used in internal combustion engines. To test the induction coil Fr Callan persuaded his students to take shocks from the output. He was eventually creating such high voltages that one of the students was put into a coma. The student, William Walsh, recovered and eventually became Archbishop of Dublin, but the college authorities stepped in and insisted Fr Callan discontinue using students in his experiments!

Navan was also the hometown of Francis Beaufort, who devised the scale of wind strengths. The Beaufort family were Huguenots,

French Protestants who fled France to escape religious persecution; in fact the word refugee was coined to describe those fleeing French harassment in the seventeenth and eighteenth centuries. In 1747 Daniel Cornelius de Beaufort arrived in Navan, where he was appointed rector of the parish, a position he held for eighteen years until he relinquished it to his son, Daniel Augustus. Daniel Augustus was a noted road-maker, mapmaker and topographer. He was also an architect and designed the new church at Navan, completed in 1818. His son, Francis, was born in 1774 and joined the Royal Navy at the tender age of fourteen. Francis received nineteen wounds when an enemy vessel was captured under the guns of a Spanish fortress. During his convalescence, he spent two years assisting his brother-in-law, Richard Lovell Edgeworth (father of Maria Edgeworth, author of *Castle Rackrent*), in the construction of a semaphore line from Dublin to Galway capable of transmitting messages across the breadth of Ireland in eight minutes. Beaufort trained Robert Fitzroy, who was in command of the survey ship HMS *Beagle* during its second voyage to South America. When Fitzroy asked him to suggest a well-educated person to go on the voyage, Beaufort's enquiries led to an invitation to Charles Darwin, who subsequently formulated his theory of evolution in *On the Origin of Species*.

Francis Beaufort is best remembered for the Beaufort Scale, which rates the winds from calm to hurricane force. A means of measuring wind speed by visual inspection of indirect factors like waves on water, the scale was devised to be used at sea in the time of sailing ships to accurately describe the speed and strength of the wind. It outlined the number of canvas sails required for each category of wind force. The scale has been revised and extended over the centuries.

Rear Admiral Sir Francis Beaufort died in 1857. The Beaufort Sea north of Alaska is named in his honour. Navan remembers his name in the Beaufort Community College, the Beaufort Mall in the shopping centre and a housing estate in the town.

Navan's most recent famous son is Pierce Brosnan, the fifth actor to play the role of James Bond. 'I'm from Navan and I'm proud to be a "Navan Man",' the actor once said. Brosnan spent much of his childhood at 2 St Finian's Terrace in the town. Born in Drogheda in 1953, he lived in Navan for his first twelve years. In 1950 his father, Tom, moved from Tralee to work in the John Hogg furniture factory. Tom met May Smith in the CYMS Hall on the Fair Green in Navan. May, who was much younger than Tom, worked in Navan Carpets. The love-struck couple married in the local church, but Tom left the family when Pierce was an infant. When Pierce was four years old, his mother moved to London to work as a nurse. From that point on he was largely brought up by his grandparents. After their deaths he lived with a grand-aunt and then another grand-aunt. He once said, 'Childhood was fairly solitary. My mother came home once or twice a year.' Brosnan was educated in the local school run by the de la Salle Brothers and served as an altar boy. It was eventually decided that he would join his mother in London, where he went on to study acting. He was made a Freeman of Navan in 1999. His local cousins are sometimes called 002, 006 and 009.

Navan local Pierce Brosnan.
Courtesy of Seamus Farrelly

Comedians Dylan Moran and Tommy Tiernan, and television personality Hector Ó hEochagáin also hail from the town.

Just outside the centre of the town, off the Athlumney road, is the Ramparts car park, which is the start of a walk along the River Boyne and the Boyne canal. This walk continues for a distance of 8 kilometres towards Slane along the banks of the River Boyne, parallel with the old canal. The Boyne Navigation Canal covered a 35-kilometre stretch of the river between Navan and Drogheda. It was unsuccessful as it was only usable for eight months of the year, there being too much water in the river during the winter months and too little in high summer. The canal barges also had to switch from one side of the river to the other, as parts of it were on different sides of the river, with the river itself being used for stretches. This made it difficult for the horses pulling the barges, as they sometimes ended up in the water in the cross-river journey. The canal was sold to the conservation body *An Taisce* in 1961 for £1. Sections are being restored, as is the canal-side walk.

Just to the southeast of Navan town, and now surrounded by housing, is Athlumney Castle, erected by the Dowdall family in the fifteenth century. The tower house succeeded an earthen motte, which still sits on the riverside. The motte and tower house were both constructed with defence as a primary objective. A fortified mansion was added to the tower house in the late sixteenth or early seventeenth century. The comfort of this building, with its large windows and fireplaces, would have contrasted with the earlier defensive tower house.

It seems that sometime in the seventeenth century the building was destroyed by fire. One story assigns the burning of the castle to Cromwell's time. Two jealous sisters were supposed to

The oriel window in Athlumney Castle.

have lived in Athlumney Castle and Blackcastle – one on either side of the Boyne. They made an agreement not to give Cromwell shelter and pledged to burn down their houses rather than let him in. When one lady set her mansion on fire that was to be the signal for the other lady to do likewise, as Cromwell was on his way. But the occupant of Blackcastle, who was jealous of the larger Athlumney, lit a fire of brushwood in one of its turrets. The lady in Athlumney, on seeing the signal, burned her house, only to discover her mistake the following morning.

A much more likely story attributes the burning to 1690. Lancelot Dowdall, the then owner, sided with King James at the Battle of the Boyne. He vowed that William, Prince of Orange, would never rest or receive shelter under his roof. As William's forces advanced, Dowdall set fire to his castle one fine evening and then calmly took his belongings across the river where he sat to watch his home burn. Throwing sparks high into the air, his home gradually disappeared into a smouldering ruin. Dowdall left for exile in France while the ashes were still hot. The gates to the castle are kept locked but there are access details on display.

At Donaghmore, to the northeast of Navan, on the Navan to Slane road, can be found a medieval round tower and church. The foundation dates to the earliest Christian period and its name is derived from the Latin word *Dominica*, which became *Domhnach* in Irish, meaning Sunday. It is said to have been blessed by St Patrick and given into the care of one of his followers, St Cassanus. The round tower dates to the tenth century. Over 30 metres tall, there were two windows at the top but these were later removed when the conical cap was replaced in the early nineteenth century. The doorway has a sculpture of the Crucifixion, with the figure of Christ crucified and on either side carvings of human heads – the two thieves.

Throughout the centuries round towers in Ireland have been ascribed to various races as it was thought that the native Irish were too dim-witted to have erected these. In the early nineteenth century Henry O'Brien published *The Round Towers of Ireland or The Mysteries of Free Masonry of Sabaism and of Budhism for the First Time Unveiled.* He declared that the figure on the Donaghmore tower was 'symbolic of the departure of Buddha'. O'Brien stated that the round towers were storehouses for idols of Buddha and were as old as the pyramids of Egypt. He concluded that the towers were 'temples constructed by the early Indian colonists of the country, in honour of that fructifying principle of nature'.

Only a small portion of the church, which was of a later date than the tower, remains standing. The graveyard at Donaghmore is extremely well kept and there is a car park.

Just off the Navan to Slane road is the castle of Dunmoe, which was based on fortresses of the twelfth and thirteenth centuries but probably not constructed until the fifteenth century. Commanding a high point over the river, the castle was built by the D'Arcy family, lords of Dunmoe. George D'Arcy, one of the burgesses of Navan recorded in the 1689 charter of King James, is supposed to have entertained James on the night before the Battle of the Boyne and King William on the night after. In this way he was sure to be seen as a supporter of the eventual winner. His willingness to switch his loyalty worked out well for him, as he managed to retain his lands when the conflict ended. It also inspired the following rhyme:

Who will be king I do not know
But I'll be D'Arcy of Dunmoe.

On the outskirts of Navan, Tara Mines is the largest lead zinc mine in Europe operating entirely underground.

The entrance to the tomb at Newgrange.
© *Shutterstock*

Newgrange, Knowth and Dowth

Set on a commanding ridge above the River Boyne, Newgrange passage grave is Ireland's most iconic archaeological site and one of the most renowned prehistoric sites in Europe. Situated in a loop or bend of the Boyne, Newgrange is part of a large complex of similar passage graves and is surrounded by smaller satellite tombs scattered throughout the nearby landscape. The immediate area, Brú na Bóinne, the palace or homestead of the Boyne, is recognised as a UNESCO World Heritage site.

The Brú na Bóinne visitor centre at Donore on the south side of the Boyne is the starting point for visits to Newgrange and Knowth; there is no direct access to these tombs. The visitor centre provides an interpretative display and an audio-visual presentation bringing the visitor back to the time these passage graves were constructed. The guided tour of Newgrange offers an opportunity to enter the passage and tomb chamber, but be aware that no photography is permitted inside the tomb. These are outdoor sites so do wear warm clothes on cold days and bring rain gear if necessary. The third of the famous Brú na Bóinne tombs, Dowth, is accessed from the north side of the Boyne.

Dating to about 3200 BC, Newgrange is a massive

Newgrange passage grave. *Courtesy of John Scarry*

mound. Constructed of alternating layers of earth and stones, it is 90 metres in diameter, covers an area of 4,400 square metres and has a ring of ninety-seven large kerbstones around the base. Over 12 metres in height, the mound covers a 19-metre passage leading to a central chamber. The name Newgrange dates from medieval times when the surrounding land became one of the outlying farms or granges of Mellifont Abbey, but the site predates the great pyramids at Giza in Egypt by some 500 years and Stonehenge by about 1,000 years and is associated with the fairy people – the Tuatha Dé Danann.

Although Newgrange is indelibly linked with the winter solstice, no one is quite sure why the Neolithic people felt the need to create such massive monuments to house their dead, or indeed if burial was the primary purpose of these monuments within the Boyne landscape. The tombs certainly would have been highly

visible, being located on low ridges above the river. According to tradition the Iron-Age high kings of Ireland were buried here, but even then Newgrange was nearly 3,000 years old.

In 1699, when Scottish settler Charles Campbell set about improving his holdings, he instructed his workmen to use Newgrange as a quarry for road-building material. As his workmen burrowed they discovered the entrance to what they described as a cave, but what was, in fact, the passage. The tomb was open freely to visitors for 200 years and some of their graffiti still marks the stones.

This enormous cairn was created by a community that worked only with stone and wood. The people who constructed these tombs must have been quite sophisticated. It would have taken an organised, highly stratified society to construct these monuments, as well as mathematical, architectural and astronomical expertise. It was the introduction of farming in Ireland during the Neolithic Age that allowed such a society to develop. With new ideas about food production guaranteeing a food supply, hunting and gathering were no longer such an important part of life. This meant more time was available for other activities and also that people started to settle in one area rather than living a nomadic lifestyle. Taking into consideration the average lifespan of Neolithic man of about thirty years, it is generally thought that the Newgrange tomb took at least two generations to construct.

The mound is surrounded by the remains of a great stone circle. Twelve standing stones survive out of a possible original thirty-five. The stone circle dates to after 2000 BC and belongs to the final phase of construction at Newgrange.

The inward-curving dark stone walls on each side of the entrance are not original and were erected to allow easy access to the passage on either side of the entrance stone. The original entrance to the passage would have been over the superbly carved front kerbstone. With its swirling spirals and lozenge shapes, this guarded the tomb's main entrance. Above the entrance is a slit, or roof box, which allows sunlight into the central chamber around the time of the winter solstice in December. Diametrically opposite the entrance stone, at the back of the mound, is the second most decorated stone at Newgrange. Excavations and surveys were carried out to investigate the possibility of a second passage from this side of the mound, but no evidence of such has been discovered.

There has been some controversy over the reconstruction of the white quartz wall that circles the front half of the tomb. It was based on the position of the white quartz layers uncovered during excavations between 1962 and 1975 and restored thus by the excavator, Professor M. J. O'Kelly. The quartz, which may have been quarried in the Wicklow mountains, is affixed to a near vertical, steel-reinforced concrete wall to keep it in position and one argument states that the pressure of the mound would have caused the quartz to collapse if it had been used this way originally. Despite criticism of the restoration, O'Kelly defended his interpretation and even carried out experiments with similar walls to see where they would fall over time, but when similar stones were found at Knowth, the excavators chose to leave them as a pavement in front of the tomb, rather than affixing them to the side. What we know for certain is that quartz is associated with both the sun and burial in Ireland; indeed the Irish word for quartz, *grianchloch*, literally translates as sun stone. Even today many modern graves are decorated with white quartz chippings.

The water-rolled granite embedded in the quartz wall came from Dundalk Bay and the Mourne mountains, both of which would have made for a considerable journey over very difficult terrain. The kerbstones and passage stones are greywacke rock either found or quarried locally. It is difficult to envisage how these large boulders were moved, as at that time horses had not yet been domesticated and the wheel had not been invented. The thousands of pebbles used to construct the mound itself were dragged from the nearby riverbed.

Entering the passage at Newgrange is like passing from one world into another. It runs 19 metres into the centre of the mound and is lined by forty-three upright stones, a number of which are engraved. Branching off the central chamber at the end of the passage are three recesses, making a cruciform design, also seen at Loughcrew, with a large basin occupying each recess. The bones of at least five people, some cremated and some un-burned, were uncovered by archaeologists within the central chamber and recesses. Perhaps these were the remains of some great kings or religious leaders. The basins would probably have held typical funerary offerings of the time, such as beads and pendants, but these were stolen long before the archaeologists arrived. The roof of the central chamber is a corbelled vault, making the tomb almost completely weatherproof. No mortar was used in construction, yet the interior has stayed bone dry for 5,000 years; some feat of engineering, particularly in the wet Irish climate.

The corbelled vault inside Newgrange. *Courtesy of John Scarry*

The large stone slabs which form the passage and which surround the base of the mound are decorated with engraved designs. These designs would have been carved on stone with stone implements probably made of flint. This megalithic art consists of lozenges, dot-in-circles, zigzags, star shapes, parallel

A decorated kerbstone from Newgrange. *Courtesy of John Scarry*

lines, spirals, diamonds, suns, concentric circles and other geometric designs. The most famous design is that of the triple spiral which is located on the right-hand stone in the central recess and is unique to Newgrange. Many attempts have been made to interpret this passage-tomb art, but the original meaning of these motifs remains unknown. They may have been symbolic, religious or magical, and it seems likely that they played a role in the ceremonies carried out at the tomb. Some of the suggestions that have been made are that the designs represent movement of the sun and stars, maps of the area, the cosmos, rebirth, reincarnation, the triumph of life over death, or even the trademark of the builders. One British newspaper even correlated the occurrence of these markings with the areas in which magic mushrooms grow!

At 8.58 a.m. on the winter solstice, 21 December, as the sun dawns over the horizon, the morning light shines through the roof box above the entrance, up the passage and into the central chamber. The passage gradually rises as it makes its way to the centre of the mound so the floor of the central chamber is at the same height as the roof box. The earth's position has changed since Newgrange was constructed and so the light now enters about four minutes after sunrise. If the day is clear the chamber is lit up for a total of seventeen minutes. This spectacle also occurs a few days before and after the solstice. Professor O'Kelly was the first person in modern times to witness this phenomenon, in 1967, although local folklore always connected the monument to the sun.

The winter solstice marks the shortest day of the year and it appears to have been a time of special significance for the people who constructed Newgrange. It marked the end of the old year and the start of the new, a time from which the days would gradually grow longer and, eventually, warmer. The Neolithic people may have viewed it as the death of the old sun and the rebirth of a new one. When the monument was excavated, a large stone was blocking the entrance to the passage, so it is not known whether humans witnessed the winter solstice from inside the tomb or not. Nowadays Christmas has replaced the winter solstice festival.

Of course, if you are lucky enough to be inside Newgrange for the solstice, there is no guarantee that there will be sunlight in the chamber on any of the mornings. The event is totally weather dependent and the skies are often overcast, so no light enters. However, it is still a special feeling to wait in the darkness, as people may have done so long ago, for the longest night of the year to end. A free lottery is held annually for tickets to the event. The draw takes place at the end of September and there are usually over 30,000 entries for just sixty places. You can enter at the visitor centre as many times as you like.

Just to the east of the tomb is a folly, the plan of which is loosely based on Newgrange. It probably dates from the eighteenth or nineteenth century and was used by the local landowner as an icehouse.

Newgrange icehouse. © *istockphoto*

The large passage grave, satellite tombs and 'woodhenge' at Knowth.

One kilometre northwest of Newgrange, at Knowth, lies a second large passage grave. When Professor George Eogan began excavating there in 1962, very little was known about the full extent of the site. It was not until 1967 that a large passage tomb was discovered in the western side of the mound; the following year the eastern passage was discovered.

The large mound that covers the two passage tombs is surrounded by over 100 massive kerbstones and comparable in size to Newgrange. Traces of at least eighteen smaller tombs surrounding the larger mound have been discovered and restored.

Two of these were constructed around 4000 BC, a thousand years before the main tomb was built.

Knowth is more complex and has a larger range of decoration than Newgrange. The decoration found there represents almost half of all acknowledged megalithic art in Ireland and nearly a third of all known megalithic art in Europe. The western passage is 34 metres long and bends at the end but there is no chamber. The eastern passage is 40 metres long, ending with a cruciform chamber similar to that at Newgrange. It was suggested that the passages were aligned towards sunrise and sunset on the spring and autumn equinoxes, but recent investigation seems to disprove this theory. Access to the passages by the public is not allowed. Instead, visitors are brought into a specially designed room within the mound where they can see the large ditch excavated as a defensive measure in the early Christian era, and also view the eastern passage. The quartz stones uncovered at Knowth have been used to form a pavement in front of the entrances to the passageways. Before each entrance stands a stone in the shape of a pillar. From the top of the mound at Knowth the site of Newgrange is easily visible.

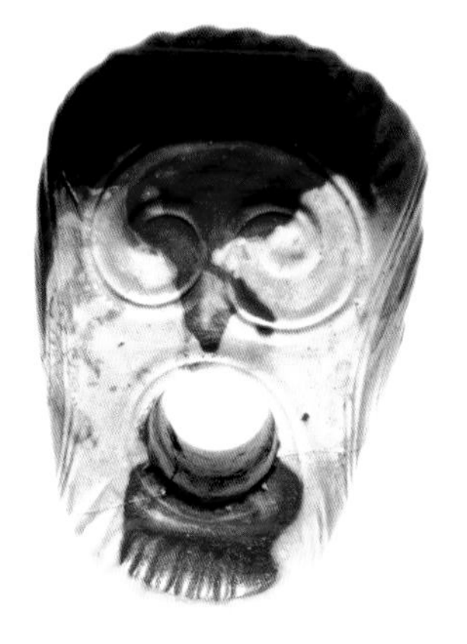

The macehead.
Courtesy of John Scarry

The excavations at Knowth continued for over forty years. Along with hundreds of pieces of pottery, jewellery and tools, a stunning flint macehead was discovered, which is currently on display at the National Museum. The macehead was created from a single piece of marbled red and white flint, polished and decorated on all six sides. The carvings resemble a stylised human face, with the shaft hole as a gaping mouth. The precision of the markings could only have been created by a rotary drill. The flint may have originated in the Orkneys and was possibly a gift or offering at Knowth. The macehead is not a functional item but was probably used in a ceremonial capacity.

Following the Iron Age the mound at Knowth was transformed. In the fifth century two huge ditches were dug at the mound, one at the base and the other on the top. Around AD 800 a residence was constructed on top of the hill for the kings of Northern Brega. An underground passage or souterrain ran from the top of the mound and may have been used as an escape route if the residence was attacked. A number of souterrains were constructed on the site between *c.* AD 750 and *c.* AD 1200, possibly for use as food storage areas. In the twelfth century the Normans created a wooden fortification on top of the mound and, later, the monks from Mellifont constructed farm buildings on the summit. When Mellifont and its granges were suppressed during the Dissolution, its lands were granted to new owners who abandoned Knowth.

Today, visitors can climb to the top of the mound, where the foundations of the twelfth-century Norman fortification are visible and they can also view the entrance to one of the souterrains. The smaller satellite mounds are not open to visitors. Outside the entrance to the eastern passage is a reconstruction of a timber circle or 'woodhenge', the original of which was constructed between 2800 and 2500 BC.

The Brú na Bóinne visitor centre houses an extensive exhibition, including a full-scale replica of the chamber at Newgrange and a model of one of the smaller tombs at Knowth. Visitors visit the exhibition and then cross the river by pedestrian bridge and take a shuttle bus to Newgrange or Knowth. At Newgrange the tour enters the chamber and the winter equinox is simulated using artificial light. It can be a tight squeeze in this small, dark chamber, so if you are in any way claustrophobic stay at the back of the group so you will not trample anyone getting out! Tickets are sold on a first come first served basis and demand for tours is very high during the summer months. It is advisable to arrive as early in the day as possible to avoid a long wait. An online booking system is also available. I recommend that you go off peak, as it will be a more pleasant experience and the guides will have more time to talk to you.

The last of the three main tombs in the Brú na Bóinne complex lies to the northeast of Newgrange. Unlike Newgrange and Knowth, the passage grave of Dowth has not undergone extensive excavations or been restored. Access to the site is free.

The name Dowth comes from *Dubad*, the Old Irish word for darkness. According to tradition the place got its name when the king of Ireland ordered all the men of the country to construct a tower to reach the heavens in one day in order to cure a plague being suffered by all the cattle in the land. But, instead, the king's sister used the tower to stop the sun in the sky so the day went on and on. The men realised they had been tricked but had to continue to work until the spell was broken, which only happened when the king and his sister slept together.

The mound at Dowth is just off a narrow country road a kilometre northeast of Newgrange and signposted off the Drogheda to Slane road. It is surrounded by a kerb of 115 stones and has two passage tombs inside it, both facing westwards. At least thirty-eight of the stones at Dowth display megalithic art, the circle being the most common motif. There is no public

access to the tombs at Dowth, although you can peer in through the metal gates that close them off. They are much less impressive than those of Knowth and Newgrange, with shorter passages and lower roofs. The south tomb has a short passage, with a circular chamber at the end and just one recess, on the right. The north tomb has a longer passage and is cruciform, with a corbelled central chamber and a number of small rooms opening off the right recess. On the days around the winter solstice the rays of the setting sun illuminate the south passage at Dowth.

In the eighteenth century a teahouse was erected on the top of the mound by Lord Netterville, so he could see into a nearby church through a telescope and 'attend' mass without being physically present. This might have allowed him to practise his religion without being subject to the anti-Catholic laws of the time. In 1847 extensive digging took place on the mound at Dowth in an attempt to find a central chamber, and explosives were used on the site. Subsequently the mound was subject to quarrying. There is now a large hollow in the top of the mound.

The mound covering the two passage tombs at Dowth.

To the east of the passage grave stands Dowth Castle, a fifteenth-century fortified tower house that has been restored. Beside it is the large, red-brick Victorian building called the Netterville Institute, which was built as an almshouse for aged women. The castle and land were bequeathed to charity by Lord Netterville, whose family had held the manor since the thirteenth century. His wishes were that 'the inmates should live in peace and good feeling with each other; and that they must be clean, tidy and perfectly sober, and that they must attend when able to those who from sickness are unable to do this for themselves'. Lord Netterville left sixty acres of land for the support of six aged women and six orphan boys.

Martin Brennan, who was a part-owner of the Netterville building for a period, challenged conventional opinion about the function of passage graves and proposed that they were in fact astronomical observatories. His books, *The Boyne Valley Vision* and *The Stones of Time*, both published in the early 1980s, continue to fascinate the general public.

Also near the mound is Dowth churchyard, in which the Fenian hero John Boyle O'Reilly is commemorated with a memorial. William O'Reilly was the master at the school in the Netterville Institute. His son, John, was born at Dowth in 1844. John joined the Irish Republican Brotherhood and was transported to Australia for the crime of treason. He escaped to America, where he became publisher of *The Pilot* newspaper, in which he opposed anti-Semitism and prejudice against African-Americans. In 1876 he organised the daring *Catalpa* rescue of six Irish Fenian prisoners from a penal colony in Fremantle, Western Australia. He is also reputed to have coined the phrase 'It is better to be Irish than to be right.'

Dowth Castle and the Netterville Institute.

Newgrange Farm, a popular place for children, is open from March to early September and features the popular Newgrange Farm Sheep Race on Sundays. It is located on the north bank of the Boyne, near the Newgrange monument and is accessed from that side of the river.

One of the Sister Houses.

Slane

Slane village, one of the most picturesque planned villages in Ireland, was designed in the eighteenth century by the local landlords, the Conyngham family. The village is erected on a steep hillside and is positioned around a crossroads where the main Dublin to Derry road intersects the Navan to Drogheda road. Although it is hard to imagine in the midst of the busy traffic of the current day, in 1788 the local parish had to appoint a constable to shoot pigs straying about the village. Four years later the constable was fined for allowing pigs to continue to wander in the street.

It is said that the four identical Georgian houses at the heart of Slane were erected for four Conyngham sisters who were extremely jealous of each other. Their father erected identical houses looking out on each other, so that each could see what the others were up to. Another tale has it that the four houses were for the local representatives of the powers in the country: the priest, the police, the doctor and the magistrate. In fact both stories are untrue, but the Conyngham family did order that all four houses be constructed to the same plan for aesthetic reasons. The four houses and four streets form an octagon, although the area is known as 'the square'.

St Patrick's Church on Chapel Street was constructed between 1798 and 1802. A decade earlier

Colonel Conyngham of Slane had been taken prisoner in France during the revolution; as a British nobleman his sentence was likely to be execution. As the trial proceeded an appeal was issued: 'Does anyone here know Colonel Conyngham?' A young priest originally from nearby Dowth, Michael O'Hanlon, spoke up and declared he knew Conyngham and his family for being remarkable in their kindness to the Irish people. Conyngham's life was spared. Some years later Fr Michael, by then parish priest of Slane, needed to replace his old church. Lord Conyngham granted a site and a donation to erect the new church. Over the west door of the building is inscribed 'Mount Charles Chapel 1802' – Earl of Mount Charles was the title given to the eldest son of the Marquess Conyngham. There was a law at the time preventing Catholics erecting belfries for their churches but in this case the rule was circumvented by building it separate from the church. This round belfry was the first Catholic belfry erected in the Diocese of Meath after the Protestant Reformation in the sixteenth century.

At the riverside stand the remains of two mills, visible from the approach to the village from the Dublin side. The main mill was developed by local landowners and an engineer with the local canal company. When it was completed in 1766 it was the largest flour mill in Ireland. Local farmers supplied the mill with wheat, which was made into flour to be sent downriver to Drogheda for export. In the twentieth century it became a textile mill, but it closed down in 1983. The Millhouse is now a wedding venue.

Slane Bridge carries the Dublin to Derry road across the Boyne and lies at the bottom of a steep hill. The original bridge dates from the fourteenth to sixteenth centuries, but major improvements were carried out on the thirteen-arch structure when the

The belfry of St Patrick's Church.

weir and mill races were constructed in 1776. The road has a sharp right-hand turn on the Slane side that has been the scene of a number of serious traffic accidents in recent years. In 1969 the brakes of a lorry laden with Bushmills and Cream of Barley whiskey failed and it crashed into the river, scattering its load on the riverbed. That night many of the bottles were 'rescued' by local people before the official divers arrived the following morning to complete the job. Apparently the local butcher was still drinking free Bushmills four years later. The actual quantity of whiskey rescued by the locals is still known only to the management of Bushmills and the insurance company.

According to tradition, it was on the Hill of Slane, right at the top of the town, that St Patrick lit the first Paschal Fire on Easter Eve in AD 433. St Patrick's fire challenged the pagan law that forbade the lighting of any other fire before the high king's fire at Tara was lit. The high king, Lóegaire, was alarmed to see a fire lit on such a prominent hill within sight of Tara. His druids

The Hill of Slane.

warned him that unless the flame was quenched it would burn forever in Ireland, a prophecy that was probably a metaphor for the spread of Christianity on the island. Patrick later made his way to Tara, where he secured the king's permission to continue preaching, although only one member of the king's retinue became Christian. Erc Mac Dega was converted by Patrick and appointed the first bishop of Slane. Erc's foundation thrived in Slane and, when he was old, he founded a hermitage on the banks of the river. St Erc lived to be ninety, engaging in day-long prayer while immersed in the river up to his neck. His favourite dinner was an egg and a half and three sprigs of watercress.

The ruins on the high point of the Hill of Slane include the remains of a parish church and walled graveyard. The long rectangular nave of the church was probably rebuilt in the thirteenth century, possibly from an earlier ninth- or tenth-century church. In the fifteenth century a bell tower was added at the west end, as was a chapel to the south of the nave. Many parishioners were apparently delighted not to have to make the journey up 'the hill of difficult ascent' after the new church was erected in the village in 1723. The gate pillar of the entrance to the graveyard has a wonderful carving of a medieval lady. Beyond the walls of the graveyard stand the remains of a college built by Christopher Fleming in 1512 and abandoned in the eighteenth century. An artificial mound on the western slope of the hill was probably the site of the first castle of the Norman family of Flemings, who settled in Slane in the twelfth century. The site provides magnificent views across the Boyne Valley, particularly of nearby Knowth and Newgrange.

Access to the hill is from the northern outskirts of the village and there is a car park beside the road. There are regular tours of the hill during the summer months and access is free all year round.

Back down on the northern bank of the Boyne, Slane Castle has been the family home of the Conyngham family since 1703. The first member of the family to come to Ireland from Scotland was Rev. Alexander Conyngham, who settled at Mountcharles in County Donegal in the seventeenth century. He and his wife had twenty-seven children but only nine survived to adulthood. Alexander's grandson, General Henry Conyngham, fought for James at the Battle of the Boyne, but when he saw how the battle was going he defected with his unit of 500 men to the other side. Another family member was already fighting on William's side. So no matter which monarch won, the Conynghams were sure to be on the winning side. The family's coat of arms is a shake-fork, and their motto *Over fork Over* is reputed to have been acquired for saving the life of King Malcolm III of Scotland by covering him in a cock of hay to conceal him from his enemies.

King Malcolm was not the only royal personage that the family were connected to. George IV of England would become intricately linked with the Conynghams. In 1795 the then Prince Regent of England married his cousin, Princess Caroline of Brunswick, in order to acquire an increased allowance from parliament. When he first saw her he called for a large brandy. When she first saw him she thought him 'very fat'. They had a tumultuous marriage, George even locking the doors of Westminster Abbey on the day of his coronation so Caroline could not enter and be crowned queen.

In August 1821, just weeks after the coronation, Caroline died and rumours quickly circulated that she had been poisoned. Days later George began an eighteen-day visit to Ireland, the first peacetime visit of any British monarch to the island. The trip was a carefully orchestrated public relations triumph and the welcome he received in Ireland was in striking contrast to his unpopularity in England. His arrival at Howth was marked by a carved imprint of his feet where he touched Irish soil for the first time, and this carving can still be viewed today. He is alleged to have imbibed an amount of Irish whiskey on board ship and was apparently in a good mood when he stumbled off the vessel.

The scandal spread that the main reason the king was visiting Ireland was to see his mistress, Elizabeth, Lady Conyngham. Elizabeth's husband had been made a marquess in 1816, possibly as a result of the affair, and went on to serve as lord steward of George's household. Legend holds that the main road from Dublin to Slane was straightened so that the king could arrive at Slane Castle quickly, but the straightening had actually been completed by 1812.

Slane Castle.

George lodged for four nights at Slane Castle from 23 to 27 August. During this time he toured the local countryside and planned a luncheon visit to nearby Annesbrook, Duleek. The owner, Mr Smith, did not have a suitable room to accommodate the king's luncheon so he had a Gothic ballroom added to his house. But on the day of the luncheon the sun shone and the king preferred to take his meal on the lawns of Annesbrook, never actually entering the house or the special room.

The king also visited Powerscourt House and was exceedingly fortunate that he left without visiting the famous waterfall. A dam had been constructed to ensure a good flow should the king arrive, but when the water was released it gushed out with such force that it washed away the specially constructed platform upon which His Majesty was due to stand.

The king departed from Dun Laoghaire, which was renamed Kingstown in his honour. Lady Conyngham remained George's mistress until his death in 1830. When George died she moved to Paris, where she lived for thirty more years. In 1837 her son, Francis, the second Marquess of Conyngham, was the person who informed Victoria that she was queen and the first to address her as 'Your Majesty'.

The current Slane Castle was principally designed around 1785 by William Burton Conyngham. One of the architects of the castle, Francis Johnston, was also responsible for the Gothic gates on the Mill Hill, near the bridge. These provided a spectacular entrance to the estate, but later fell out of use. Inside the castle the round ballroom, completed in 1821 and possibly designed by Thomas Hopper, an architect favoured by George IV, has a superb fan-vaulted ceiling.

U2 recorded their album 'The Unforgettable Fire' at the

castle in 1984. In 1991 a real, unforgettable fire in the castle caused extensive damage to the building and completely gutted the eastern section facing the river. A third of the building was destroyed and the rest severely damaged. After the completion of a restoration programme, the castle re-opened in 2001 and tours of the interior are available. It is also possible to tour Slane Whiskey Distillery, in the grounds of the castle, which provides an opportunity for visitors to immerse themselves in the process of making whiskey, from grain to glass.

Slane Castle's sloping lawns form a natural amphitheatre and so it has become the venue for major pop and rock concerts. Set against the stunning backdrop of the River Boyne and the surrounding parkland of the estate, it is an impressive venue. The open-air amphitheatre has an 80,000-person capacity. Internationally renowned acts who have headlined Slane concerts since 1981 include The Rolling Stones, David Bowie, Eminem, Guns N' Roses, Bon Jovi, U2, Queen, Red Hot Chilli Peppers, Bob Dylan, Bruce Springsteen, Oasis, Neil Young, Bryan Adams, Robbie Williams, Madonna and R.E.M.

The parklands around the castle were laid out by the distinguished landscape architect, Capability Brown. Brown dispatched plans for the landscape from England and despite receiving many invitations to come to work in Ireland, he is supposed to have replied that he had 'not yet finished England'. These parklands can be visited when the castle is open.

Just east of the village, on the Drogheda road, is the Francis Ledwidge Museum. Ledwidge, the famous Slane poet, was born in 1887. Leaving school at the age of fourteen he worked in various manual labour positions while developing a love for poetry, drawing on the beauty of the Boyne valley for inspiration.

The writer Lord Dunsany became his patron. Despite being a nationalist, on the outbreak of the First World War Ledwidge enlisted in the same regiment as Dunsany, the Royal Inniskilling Fusiliers. He later explained, 'I joined the British Army because she stood between Ireland and an enemy of civilisation and I would not have her say that she defended us while we did nothing but pass resolutions.' Another reason for his decision was that he had been rejected by a local girl, Ellie Vaughey.

The Ledwidge Museum.

An initial volume of fifty of Ledwidge's poems, *Songs of the Field*, was published in 1915, while he was serving. Ledwidge was part of the force assigned to fight the Turks and he arrived in Gallipoli in July 1915, where he saw action at Suvla Bay. Ledwidge injured his back during the retreat to Salonika and was convalescing in a military hospital in Manchester when he heard news of the Easter Rising and the execution of its leaders. He had admired Patrick Pearse and James Connolly, while Thomas

MacDonagh had been a personal friend. After their executions he observed, 'If someone were to tell me now that the Germans were coming in over our back wall, I wouldn't lift a finger to stop them. They could come!'

In December 1916 Ledwidge was posted to Amiens. The third battle of Ypres began on 31 July 1917. On that day a group from Ledwidge's battalion were road-laying in preparation for an assault. While Ledwidge was drinking tea in a mud hole with his comrades, a random shell exploded alongside, killing the poet and five others. A chaplain who knew him, Fr Devas, arrived soon after and recorded, 'Ledwidge killed, blown to bits.'

Matt McGoona, a friend of Ledwidge, was a printer at the *Meath Chronicle* in Navan. On the day his friend was killed he was working at the newspaper when he heard the familiar sound of Ledwidge arriving on his motorcycle. When he dashed outside, there was Ledwidge in motorcycle gear. But as McGoona approached him, Ledwidge and the motorbike disappeared. A few days later a telegraph arrived bearing the news of Ledwidge's death at the same time as he had appeared to his friend in Navan.

The small museum is a perfect example of a labourer's cottage. It houses the poet's works and artefacts from the First World War.

Another museum in the vicinity well worth a visit is the Irish Military War Museum, situated on the road to Collon. This is Ireland's only museum where you can handle the weaponry, and it specialises in First and Second World War material. The museum recreates examples of trenches from the First World War, as well as displays of the highly motorised conflict that was the Second World War. Visitors can even learn to drive a tank, an original FV432 armoured personnel carrier.

St Patrick's Church.

Tara

Free to the public, with a great wide open space for kids to run wild on, Tara is a magical place – there you can walk in the footsteps of saints and heroes. The legendary seat of the high kings of Ireland, Tara has been an icon of Irish nationhood for centuries and every decade or so it is suggested as the location for a neutral capital of a united Ireland. In 1942 an architect even drew up plans for the new city of Tara, with a parliament, cathedral, museum, theatre, airport and university.

Thomas Moore's melody 'The Harp that Once through Tara's Halls' is suggestive of an immense palatial past for Tara. Located just off the Navan to Dunshaughlin road, there are no signs of such a regal past, nor any impressive buildings, only simple earthworks, most of which appear only as humps and hollows in the ground. But if you know the stories this landscape will come alive for you. Tara, the home of the legends, was peopled with druids famed for their wizardry, judges wise in judgement, warriors brave in battle, bards and minstrels. A great assembly place, the hill is associated with legendary people like the leader of the Fianna Fionn Mac Cumhaill, Niall of the Nine Hostages, Queen Maeve, Conn of the Hundred Battles, and Diarmuid and Gráinne. To really appreciate Tara it is necessary to use your imagination to see again the heroes and kings of old.

Although just over 150 metres in height, the hill of Tara commands the surrounding countryside, and views right across the plains of Ireland can be observed from the summit. On a clear day it is claimed that it is possible to see half the counties of Ireland: to the northeast are the Mountains of Mourne and to the south are the Dublin and Wicklow mountains. To the east is the Hill of Skryne, to where St Colmcille's bones were moved for safekeeping from attacks by the Vikings on Iona. The name Skryne is derived from *Scrin Choluim Chille*, the shrine of Colmcille. The large building that can be seen to the north of Tara is Dalgan Park, the home of the Columban missionaries who sent priests to China and the Far East. Many were tortured, some to death, when the communists took over China. There are some lovely walks in the grounds of Dalgan; access is off the Tara to Navan road, with plenty of parking at the building.

Tara from the air. *Courtesy of Aubrey Martin*

Also visible to the east of Tara, in the valley below, is the farmyard of the house of Lord Tara, John Brabazon. He won a prize in 1910 for being the first British pilot to fly more than one mile.

Tara has been an important site from the Neolithic period. The buildings on the site would have been made of mud and wattle and these have returned to the earth. But the dramatic slopes and changes in ground level of the rings and mounds that survive can be appreciated by a stroll around the ancient grassy landscape, although aerial photographs give the best idea of how the site looks overall.

The *Annals of the Four Masters* record that Tara was a place of ritual and ceremony, particularly in the fifth to eight centuries AD, but most of the surviving monuments date back to the Bronze and Early Iron Ages. The name Tara has three possible derivations: sanctuary or sacred area; the place of the great height; or taken from a mythological queen named Tea. The names currently given to the monuments on the hill were recorded many centuries after Tara was deserted, and written by Christians who did not approve of the pagan past which the site represented.

It was said that he who ruled Tara, ruled Ireland. After the site was abandoned, records were compiled which claimed that more than 140 Celtic kings reigned in the name of Tara. It is important to note that the high kingship was not hereditary and different families from all over the country held the royal position at one time or another. To be the proven king one had to submit to a test. The chosen man sat on the Stone of Destiny and if the stone roared then this was the true king. If the stone remained silent then the man was an imposter. The kings were not normally resident at Tara and may only have visited on special or ritual occasions.

There is continuing discussion as to what being the high king of Ireland meant. Claiming to be the high king did not actually give you power over the entire island, and the role may have been that of a lawgiver or religious figure. According to tradition every three years a festival or feis was held at Tara at the time of Samhain, which may have had an administrative or religious purpose. Kings throughout Ireland, including the high king, were closely connected to the goddess of the land, or earth mother, and when there was a harmonious relationship between them the land prospered. This connection was celebrated in different formats. In the twelfth century the inauguration rights of the kings of Donegal were recorded. A white mare was killed and boiled in water, and a bath prepared in this water for the new

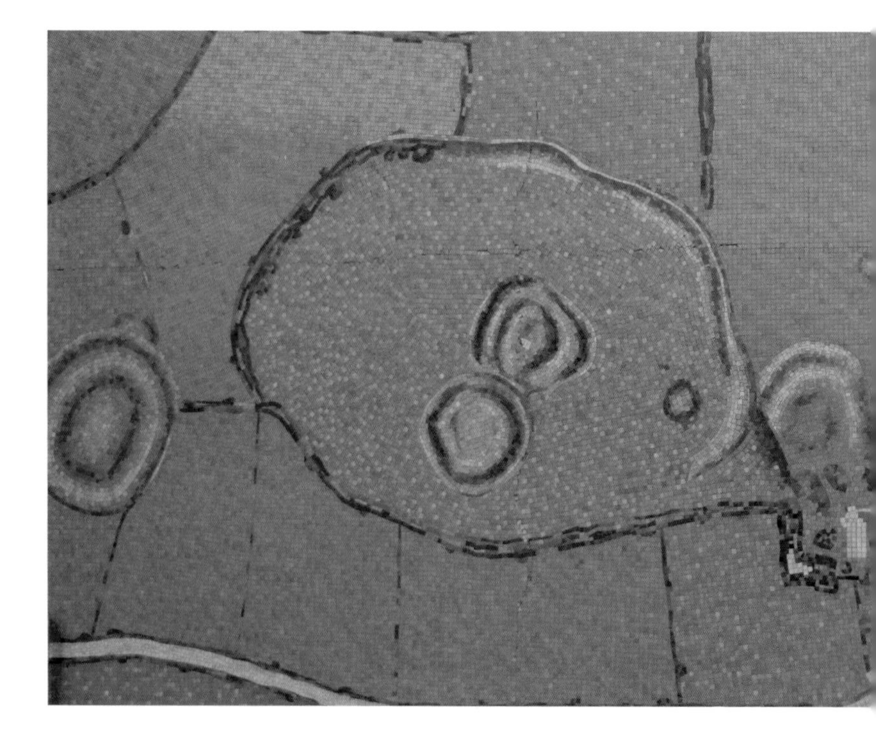

king. He would get into the pot and eat the flesh of the mare, with his people standing around and sharing it with him. He also drank the water in which he was bathing, not from a cup, nor with his hand, but only with his mouth. The inauguration rites at Tara could have been similar, as horse bones were discovered at Tara during excavations in 1997 and knife marks on the bones show that horses were butchered and eaten. A number of local place names are also derived from the Irish words for white mare.

The sightseer is first greeted by a modern statue of St Patrick, which stands outside the walls of the visitor centre. This is a traditional view of Patrick, complete with bishop's mitre, an article of clothing not used until hundreds of years after his death. An older statue once stood further up the hill but was removed as it

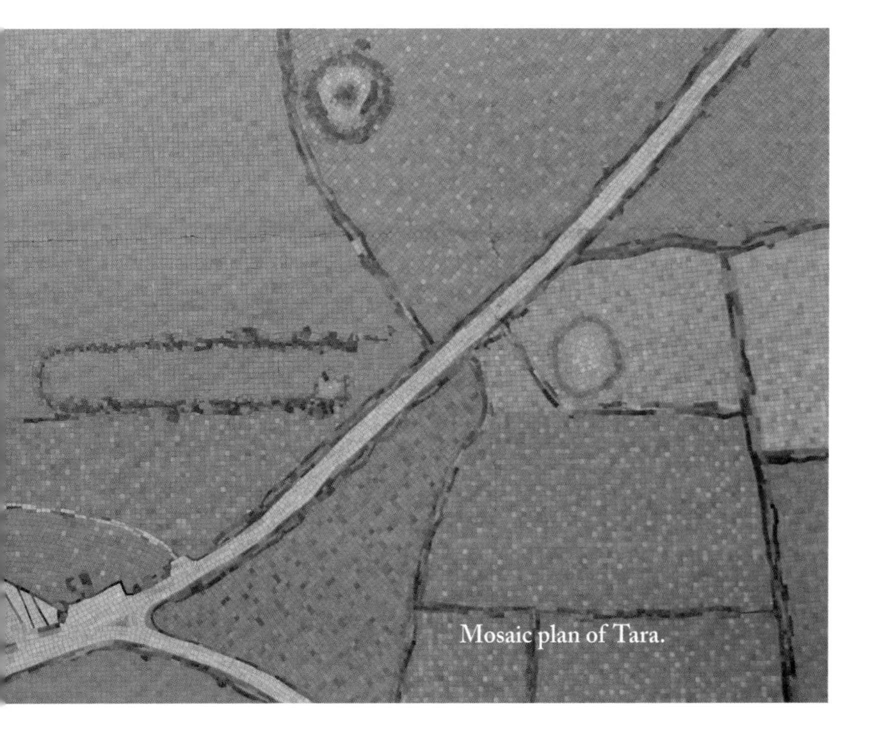

Mosaic plan of Tara.

The statue of St Patrick at Tara.

was badly damaged. According to tradition, Patrick lit the Paschal fire on the Hill of Slane to the northeast and came to Tara to explain Christianity. It was also on Tara that St Patrick was said to have used the shamrock to demonstrate the concept of the Trinity, three leaves yet one leaf, three parts to one God. The shamrock remains the national symbol of Ireland and is used as the emblem of Ireland throughout the world, except in Germany where a food processor got there first and trademarked the logo as their own.

The visitor centre is a converted church dedicated to the saint. The church, which dates to 1822, has a wonderful stained-glass window. Created by Evie Hone, the east window, with images of Pentecost interspersed with images of St Patrick on the Hill of Tara, was erected to mark the 1,500th anniversary of St Patrick's arrival in and mission to Ireland. Each year the local Church of Ireland community holds an open-air service with music provided by one of the local silver bands. In the churchyard outside are two standing stones, one with a male figure possibly representing the Celtic fertility god Cernunnos.

To get a real sense for the layout of the ancient site, you should start your visit at the so-called Banqueting Hall, to the right of the church. Aligned to the Mound of the Hostages, this consists of two parallel banks over 200 metres in length. This monument received its name from the *Book of Leinster*, where it was described and drawn almost 1,000 years ago. The plan of the hall depicts hostages located close to a fire where they would be in everybody's view, rather than at the back of the hall where they could perhaps plan an escape. According to stories, at the centre of the hall was a big cauldron able to hold an entire cow, pig and sheep. Each portion of the meat was allocated to the attendance, so it is likely that the king got the steak while the guard at the back door got the shin of the pig.

However, the Banqueting Hall was most likely the ceremonial entrance to the holy site of Tara. Archaeologists now believe it was a processional avenue or cursus, a Neolithic structure which was probably used for ceremonial purposes. This type of monument is rare in Ireland but common in southern Britain. Gaps in the parallel banks on either side are thought to be for providing views of significant sites. Walking between the two banks, up the hill to the sacred site, must have created quite an impression, the apprehension rising as the subject neared the holy of holiest places on top of the hill. A similar trick was used by Mussolini, a small man who had a huge desk placed at the end of a huge room, so that by the time someone reached the desk they felt intimidated by the scale of the place.

Once through the Banqueting Hall you reach the Rath of the Synods, named thus because it was the site of three meetings

Looking up the Banqueting Hall.

of churchmen who made changes to the laws of Ireland. At the final synod held here St Ruadán cursed Tara – 'May Tara be desolate forever.' The story was that the high king had abused the sanctuary of Ruadán's monastery by removing an outlaw from its precincts. Ruadán foretold that Tara would be deserted and that it would be grazed by sheep. Nowadays no one lives on Tara and sheep, which are light enough not to do any damage to the archaeological remains, are used to keep the grass down. Tara was such a significant pagan centre that the only way to prevent its influence continuing was to curse it.

Current evidence indicates that the Rath of the Synods was originally a third- or fourth-century BC open-air temple surrounded by large wooden beams, later converted into a burial ground. In 1810 a boy digging close to the rath discovered two magnificent gold torcs which are now in the National Museum in Dublin. Dating from around 1200 BC, the torcs are too large for a king's neck and may have decorated wooden idols.

In 1899 this rath was excavated by a cult, the British Israelites, who thought the Ark of the Covenant was buried there. The British Israelites believed they were the lost tribe of Israel, that they were the chosen people. Destroying the Rath of the Synods, all they discovered were some rock trenches and a number of bracelets, which they threw into the Boyne. They also uncovered a number of wooden boxes deliberately buried there for them to find by their landlord, Gussy Briscoe. Apparently a curse would fall on whoever found the Ark, so when a digger came upon one of these wooden boxes everyone scarpered and only came back when they thought it was safe. Briscoe would also go up and bury pieces of coal for them to find. Each time they found something it meant that they would stay for longer, so Briscoe got another week's rent. Briscoe lived at Bellinter House, which is visible from the hill to the northwest. He is best known for riding his horse from the cellars to the attic of his house to win a bet. Horses are fine going up but not so good going down, and the poor animal had to spend a week in the attic before a pulley could be constructed to get it back to ground level.

There is a man who lives in Kells, a modern-day British Israelite, who claims to know exactly where the Ark of the Covenant is buried on the Hill of Tara, but the government, which now owns the land, has refused him permission to dig on this important archaeological site.

The Rath of the Synods was re-excavated by archaeologists led by Seán P. Ó Ríordáin and Rúaidhrí de Valera in the 1950s, and a number of Roman artefacts were uncovered. Excavations produced Roman material from the first and second centuries AD, which could prove a connection between the royals of Tara and the Roman world.

Beyond the Rath of the Synods is Rath na Rí, the Royal Enclosure, which encircles a number of the monuments on the hill. Constructed in the Iron Age about 100 BC, it is an oval enclosure, measuring 1 kilometre in circumference. The bank and ditch which surround it were clearly not defensive, as if they had been the ditch would be outside the bank, not inside. This arrangement is mirrored at the ritual site of Navan Fort in Armagh.

Crossing the boundary of Rath na Rí a visitor arrives at the oldest monument on the hill. The Mound of the Hostages, dating to about 3350 BC, is a megalithic passage tomb. It marks the beginning of Tara's role as a burial site. One of the most famous names associated with Tara is Niall of the Nine Hostages, which is presumably the source of the mound's name. Any hostages that were held at Tara would have been very different from our vision of hostages today: they were treated as honoured guests provided the political group they represented behaved.

The tomb's passage is short and aligned to sunrise on the cross-quarter days of 8 November and 4 February, during the ancient festivals of Samhain and Imbolc (the first day of spring). Just inside the entrance, on the left, is a large stone decorated with concentric circles, dots, swirls and cup marks. A collection of burnt and unburnt human bone, representing over 300 individuals buried between 3350 and 3100 BC, was uncovered during the archaeological investigation in the 1950s. About a thousand years later the passage and mound were used for individual cremation burials where the remains were contained in pottery urns. A highly decorated axe head, now in the National Museum, probably dates from this period. More than thirty-five Bronze Age (2500–500 BC) burials were inserted into the mound. A young man of about fourteen or fifteen, with a necklace of jet, amber, earthenware and bronze beads, was buried within the

The Mound of the Hostages.

mound and at his feet were a dagger and bronze awl. His bones were carbon-dated to between 1700 and 1600 BC. The presence of amber suggests trading connections with Scandinavia or the Baltics, while the nearest source of jet is northeast England.

Directly in front of the Mound of the Hostages is the Forrad or royal seat, a large flat-topped mound protected by two ditches. At the centre of the Forrad stands the Lia Fáil, the Stone of Destiny. It is reputed to shriek when touched by the rightful king of Tara. But how could a stone do this? A medieval manuscript describes how Conaire Mór, at his inauguration as high king, drove his chariot so close to the stone that the axle rubbing off the stone made a loud shrieking noise. Driving a chariot at such a speed at a large stone to create such a noise while avoiding a serious accident would have necessitated being either very brave or very stupid! To be declared high king, a man had to be pure in mind, body and spirit. If he was missing any part of his body, he was automatically ineligible.

Other legends are also connected to this stone. Some say it was the pillow of Jacob; others consider it to have been a fertility symbol. It is said that the original stone was taken to Scotland, where it was renamed the Stone of Scone and used as a coronation stone by the first Scottish king, Fergus Mac Erc. Edward I of England moved the Stone of Scone to Westminster, where it remained under the throne until recent decades.

The Lia Fáil was moved from near the Mound of the Hostages to its current position to mark the graves of 400 rebels who died at the Battle of Tara and are said to be buried there; it also seems to have been marked with a cross at that time. The battle was part of a rebellion that broke out in Ireland in 1798, inspired by the ideals of liberty, equality and fraternity. The rebels in Meath assembled on the Hill of Tara. They numbered about 4,000 and faced a much smaller government force of about 500 men. But the rebels were poorly led and poorly armed with swords, scythes, pitchforks and pikes, while the government force was well armed and trained. It also possessed a small cannon and a unit of cavalry. The men on both sides were mostly Irish; the government yeomanry was captained by the Catholic Lord Fingall of nearby Killeen. Allegedly three cartloads of whiskey from a Navan distillery were deliberately diverted by the government force to the road which ran by Tara. The inevitable happened, the whiskey was captured by the rebels and drunk.

The rebels had gathered around the church on the top of the hill and so had a defensive advantage, but at the start of the battle they left their strong position and charged downhill. The armed yeomen opened fire and drove the rebels back. Another charge was repulsed by cannon fire and eventually the surviving rebels broke and ran. The cavalry unit was then brought to bear to wipe out any remaining pockets of resistance. Just thirty government troops were killed.

Two memorials commemorate the Battle of Tara, one near the Lia Fáil in the Forrad and a granite Celtic cross to its north. It is interesting that when foreign help came to Ireland during our rebellions it always seemed to arrive at the worst destination possible. In 1798 most of the action was in the southeast and northeast of the country, yet the French landed on the west coast. In 1601, when Hugh O'Neill was fighting in the north, the Spanish landed at Kinsale, on the south coast.

Cormac's House, which abuts the Forrad, is described by archaeologists as a ringfort, a domestic settlement from the first millennium AD. Its position within Rath na Rí and attached to

The Lia Fáil and 1798 memorial.
© *Shutterstock*

the Forrad suggests that the people residing there considered themselves to be of high status. The name is taken from Cormac Mac Airt, one of the legendary high kings who reputedly ruled from Tara. As a young prince he gave a famous judgement when sheep belonging to a local farmer broke into the queen's garden and ate her woad plants. The queen demanded the sheep in recompense for the damage caused. The king as judge agreed, but Cormac spoke up: 'Shear the sheep and give the wool to the queen, the queen's woad like the sheep's wool will grow back. One shearing for another.'

To the west of the Forrad, on the slope of the hill, can be seen the Fairy Tree. The hawthorn or whitethorn tree is associated

The Fairy Tree.
© *Shutterstock*

with the fairies and the little people, and in recent times visitors have started to leave an offering for the fairies in the form of a ribbon or piece of cloth tied to Tara's tree in exchange for a wish.

To the south of the royal enclosure lies another late Bronze or early Iron Age ringfort, Ráth Lóegaire, where the king it is named after is alleged to have been buried in an upright position with his shield and full arms, prepared to defend his palace and the kingdom of Midhe against the Leinstermen even in death.

Another rath can be found to the west of the Banqueting Hall – Rath Gráinne – and beyond a line of trees to the west of this, two ring barrows called the Sloping Trenches cling to the hill's steep western incline. These burial barrows are quite large and incorporate older burial monuments into their rings. The name Rath Gráinne recalls the great Irish love story of the daughter of Cormac Mac Airt, Gráinne, and Diarmuid. Gráinne was betrothed to the king's elderly commander, Fionn Mac Cumhaill, but fell in love with one of his young warriors, Diarmuid, and forced him to elope with her. The enraged Fionn and the Fianna followed their trail around the country. The couple could not eat where they cooked, or sleep where they ate – they had to keep moving if they were to stay ahead of their pursuers. Eventually Fionn and Diarmuid made peace, but the tale ends tragically, with a wild boar killing Diarmuid.

To explain the unusual location of the Sloping Trenches, legend has it that they were created when the palace of Lugaid Mac Conn, a bad king, collapsed, after his judgements were shown to be false by a young Cormac Mac Airt.

As well as being the site of the Battle of Tara, this ancient place would again play an important role in the struggle for Irish freedom when, in 1843, Daniel O'Connell held one of his monster meetings there. These were part of his campaign against the union of Ireland and Great Britain. The meeting attracted nearly a million people and there was no amplification system! In 1916 Tara once again was designated as the meeting place of the rebels of Meath and Louth.

Exciting new research and excavations by the Hill of Tara Discovery Programme research team continue to add to our understanding of this unique site. Many of its secrets remain hidden and surveys have shown that under the soil are at least twice the number of monuments as those that are visible.

Outside the site, down the road from the shop, is a stone-covered well called St Patrick's Well. Originally this was a pagan well called the Well of the White Cow and its water was believed to have healing properties. It was a common Christian practice to rename wells dedicated to pagan deities with saints' names and incorporate their prayers into the existing rituals – Christianity adapted itself to the Irish way of doing things.

Half a mile south of the Hill of Tara is another hillfort, Rath Maeve, the fort of the legendary Queen Maeve, who is more usually associated with Connacht. It is an immense late Neolithic/early Bronze Age embanked enclosure measuring 230 metres in diameter, but there is not much left of this site beyond the large, overgrown earth embankment.

One of Ireland's most famous Celtic artefacts takes its name from Tara: the Tara Brooch, currently on display in the National Museum, Dublin. However, it was actually found near the seashore at Bettystown, County Meath, in 1850. It was named the Tara Brooch rather than the Bettystown Brooch because Tara was so well known and the name resonated with people, meaning that copies could be sold at a higher price; in other words this was a marketing ploy. Queen Victoria ordered two copies of the brooch for herself and the penannular brooch is often replicated in modern Irish jewellery.

In the early 2000s it was proposed to lay a new motorway, the M3, through the Tara valley. This proposal was the subject of many protests and much controversy. The discovery of a wooden Iron Age henge, possibly a ceremonial enclosure or temple, on the site of the road at Lismullin further escalated tensions, and Irish scholars and academics worldwide opposed the motorway. Despite this, it went ahead and opened in 2010.

Tara is free to visit all year round and twenty-four hours a day. Despite the numbers of visitors it is still possible to be alone and commune with the ancient stories on parts of the hill. It can be a wild and windy spot, and when the wind is blowing make sure to wrap up warm. There is a free parking area which fills up quickly, so prepare for some driving with cars parked on the narrow access road. Maguire's shop has a café and many interesting books and items. Toilets are also part of the shop complex. The church, which now houses the interpretive centre where a presentation on Tara's history is provided, along with tours of the site, is only open for the summer months.

The Russian cannon outside the walls of Trim Castle.

Trim

Although the heritage town of Trim is dominated by medieval ruins, the town's foundation dates back to the fifth century AD, when a nephew of St Patrick, Loman, founded a church near the ford of Trim. *Bhaile Átha Truim*, the town's Irish name, means the town of the ford of the elder trees. A ford was a shallow place for crossing a river, and many settlements grew up around such vital points of communication.

However, it was the coming of the Normans in the twelfth century which would have the greatest impact on this Irish town and create a legacy that has led to Trim regularly being listed as one of the top tourist attractions in Ireland. It became the site of the largest castle in Ireland, as well as seven monasteries and three hospitals. This medieval legacy of buildings is not equalled anywhere else in Ireland.

But the history of the site is older than the castle and older even than Loman. Excavations in the green space to the south of the castle uncovered a number of pig bones dated to 370–110 BC. The deposit consisted almost entirely of forelegs. There were fifty-one pig forelegs, which could have been votive offerings deposited as part of a ritual feast, or part of an autumn slaughter. What happened to the rest of the pigs' carcasses is not known.

The Anglo-Normans arrived in Ireland in the

late 1160s. In 1172 Hugh de Lacy was granted the kingdom of Meath by King Henry II, and the following year de Lacy constructed a castle at Trim to oversee his lordship. The site chosen was at a convenient crossing on the River Boyne and in the centre of his huge grant. The first castle was a ringwork castle, a wooden structure surrounded by a defensive earthwork, timber palisade and external ditch, which was quickly succeeded by the stone castle. The date of construction of the stone castle at Trim remained a matter for discussion amongst academics until the late 1990s, when tree rings from timbers in the castle wall were used to firmly date the initial construction to 1174–5. The timbers were found in the square holes that can be seen in the castle walls – putlock holes – which held large pieces of timber on which scaffolding for the initial construction of the castle was erected. Originally painted white, the castle must surely have been designed to intimidate both the native Irish and the de Lacy subordinates.

Hugh de Lacy was killed by an O'Kearney at Durrow in 1186. Former American President Barack Obama's Irish ancestor was an O'Kearney from that particular area. Walter de Lacy succeeded his father as lord of Meath. However, the de Lacy family became too independent and when Walter gave shelter to his father-in-law, William de Braose, who had fallen out of favour with King John, the family's relationship with the crown soured. In 1210 John came to Ireland to reinforce his rule. Walter and his brother fled to France but were later reinstated. The castle is sometimes called King John's Castle, even though when John was in Trim he pitched his tents on the far side of the river, rather than taking up residence in the castle.

In 1465 the country was in such a state of unrest that a

Trim Castle.

parliament held at Trim authorised the killing and beheading of all robbers, or those thought to be going stealing. A bounty on each head was to be paid by the portrieffe (mayor) of Trim. The heads were to be placed on spikes on the walls of the castle, where they would be left until they decomposed and the skull fell into the moat. Birds would come along and collect hair for building their nests and crows would pluck out the juicy eyeballs to eat.

In the 1970s an archaeological dig in the grounds of the castle uncovered the remains of ten men who had been beheaded. Two of the skeletons showed that the axeman had to strike at least twice before severing the head fully. One of the recovered skulls showed that when the axeman was about to drop his weapon the prisoner raised his head and the axe hit the back of his head. Trim's motto then, as now, was 'Always Welcome the Visitor'.

Unlike other castle sites, where the buildings were redesigned and rebuilt every few hundred years by their occupying families, Trim remained largely unchanged from the thirteenth century. This is because the families who owned this particular castle kept dying out, or marrying into more important families, which meant Trim itself was neglected. The lack of change means that it is the best-preserved Anglo-Norman castle in the country.

Trim Castle consists of a triangular enclosure of curtain walls defended by flanking towers, with a large keep in the centre. The main part of the castle, the keep, was a twenty-sided structure, cruciform in shape. No other castle has a plan similar to this – again de Lacy may have been trying to impress. The keep was surrounded by a ditch, the long curtain wall and, outside the wall, a moat. The water supply for the moat came from the 'Leper Stream', named after a leper hospital about 200 metres out the Dublin road at The Maudlins. In medieval times there were about a dozen leper hospitals scattered around the country; one gave its name to Leopardstown, a suburb of Dublin.

Conditions within the keep would have been smelly. At the base of the west tower of the keep is a stone-lined pit where toilet waste was collected, having fallen through the chutes in the garderobes, down the side of the castle and into the pit. The garderobe gives its name to the modern wardrobe, as it was there that the inhabitants of the castle also kept their clothes. The smell and the fumes rising from the pit outside kept the clothes free of lice and other infestations. If there were not enough fumes coming up, a man, the gong-scourer, also called a stirrer, was designated to stir the pit. Moreover, the people themselves only washed once a year, whether they needed it or not.

Inside the keep were three storeys of living quarters for the family, while the Great Hall, used for major events such as feasts, and a small chapel were to be found in the castle yard along with a royal mint which produced Irish coinage named 'Patricks' and 'Irelands'. Only the keep survives above ground level today.

The outer or curtain walls went all the way around the castle and enclosed over three acres. On the southern side are five D-shaped towers. The south or Dublingate is unique in Ireland as it is the only complete tower and barbican in the country. The main tower is circular in shape and approximately 10 metres in diameter. It is placed astride the curtain wall and within it is the groove for a portcullis. When raised, the drawbridge cut off the inner gate from the entrance in the barbican. Access to this raised outer gateway was probably by means of an earthen ramp. The arch under the barbican spanned the moat.

The wide moat was used as a repository for castle waste. On the side of the Dublingate tower is a sluice through which the inhabitants dumped household and toilet waste. Every few years the moat filled up and had to be cleaned out.

The side of the wall facing the Boyne, little of which survives, measured 178 metres and was defended by four flanking towers.

The town gate of the castle, now the gate through which visitors enter, has a protecting 'murder hole' where the defenders could pour boiling oil or water on anyone attempting to break

The walls and Dublingate of Trim Castle.

through the wooden portcullis. The 'murder hole' and the grooves for the portcullis or sliding gate can still be seen. Originally this gateway had been protected by a rectangular barbican, which has since been destroyed. To the left of the gate was the dungeon or *oubliette,* which has been converted into office space for the tour service in the castle. The oubliette gets its name from the French word, *oublier*, which means to forget. This dungeon consisted of a square hole with no stairs: the prisoners were thrown in there and forgotten.

There are three sally-ports in the walls of the castle, two at the front facing the church and one near the river. These small gates at the base of the wall were used by defenders to make a secret escape if the castle was under siege.

In 1993 the castle was purchased by the state and the following year became a set for the film *Braveheart*. The movie starred Mel Gibson as the Scottish hero William Wallace, with Sophie Marceau, Patrick McGoohan, Brendan Gleeson and a host of well-established Irish actors among the cast. Hundreds of Trim locals were employed as extras. Outside the castle walls was transformed into the thirteenth-century city of York which was besieged by the Scots in the movie. The keep inside the walls stood in for the Tower of London, where Wallace was executed in 1305. A local story has it that one of the extras on the set was over-enthusiastic when it came to throwing apples at Wallace as he was pulled along to his execution. When Gibson was hit with a good hard throw, the actor leaped up and let people know how he felt. When the lunch break that day dragged on for more than the usual hour, the extras discovered that Gibson was going through the film rushes in an attempt to find out who threw the apple, but the culprit was never officially identified. The keep also appeared in the scene where Edward I kills his son's lover by throwing him out of a window.

The grounds and the keep are open during most of the year and there is an admission charge. Access to the keep is by guided tour only.

The Russian cannon situated in the castle grounds was captured by the British forces in the Crimean War in the middle of the nineteenth century. The cannon bears the Tzar's coat of arms – a double-headed eagle. Most of these cannons came from the besieged port of Sebastopol, which fell to the British and French in September 1855, revealing a huge arsenal of ordnance stored in artillery parks and foundries around the city. In Trim, when the proposal was put at the local government meeting to display one of the captured cannons, one person declared, 'We do not want this symbol of British imperialism!' However, when it was realised that Ennis, Athy, Galway and other towns were getting one or more, the cry became 'We want one too.'

Beside the castle, near Trim Castle Hotel, stands a sculpture created from bog oak. Entitled *A Hunger for Knowledge*, this 2,000-year-old piece of wood recalls the well-loved traditional tale of the salmon of knowledge. This salmon was a magical fish which lived in a pool in the River Boyne. The first person to taste the fish would acquire all the knowledge of the world. An elderly bard, Finnegas, devoted his life to catching the fish and eventually hauled the salmon out onto the riverbank. Exhausted by the struggle, he instructed his apprentice, Fionn, to cook the fish. As the fish cooked a blister arose on the side and Fionn thrust in his thumb to burst it. As he did so a particle of the fish burned onto his thumb and he naturally reacted by putting it into his mouth, thereby acquiring the knowledge for himself. Fionn later went on to be a great hero, head of the high king's army and the greatest thumbsucker in history. The inscriptions on the sculpture relate to the work of a local famous mathematician, William Rowan Hamilton, on quaternions.

A short walk from the castle is St Patrick's Catholic Church, the foundation stone for which was laid in 1891 by Dr Nulty, the Bishop of Meath. The altars are the work of Pearse and Sons of Dublin; one of the sons was Patrick Pearse, one of the leaders of the 1916 Rising. The sanctuary mosaics are based on illustrations in the *Book of Kells*. There are two intentional mistakes. On the floor St Peter has five fingers and a thumb on one hand, and on the rear wall one tree has a leaf which is falling, while on the other side of the altar the leaf is in its proper place. This is to show that the work was created by imperfect man, not the great creator himself. The two major windows in the north and south transepts depict St Patrick on Tara and the statue of Our Lady of Trim.

Beside St Patrick's Church, and with a large wall facing the castle, are the remains of the new gaol of Trim, erected in 1834.

Facing Trim Castle across the Boyne, at the edge of the Porchfields, are the remains of the Augustinian monastery of St Mary's, which is also called Talbot's Castle. The abbey was founded in the twelfth century. The Yellow Steeple, the bell tower of the abbey, takes its name from the golden colour of the stonework at sunset. This tower was supposedly destroyed by the guns of Cromwell's army, a scene illustrated in a stained-glass window in St Patrick's Catholic Church. A wooden bridge which connects the south bank with the Porchfields allows access to the Yellow Steeple, as well as to Sheepgate and to a path that runs along the riverbank to the ruins at Newtown.

St Mary's was the centre of great medieval pilgrimages to

the miraculous statue of Our Lady of Trim. The *Annals of the Four Masters* record that in 1444 'Great miracles [were] worked through St Mary's Image in Ath Truim to wit, gave his eyes to the blind, his tongue to the dumb, his legs to the cripple or lame and the reaching of his hand to one that had it tied to his side

St Mary's Abbey and the Yellow Steeple.

and cats brought forth by a big bellied woman that was thought to be with child.' Giving birth to cats or animals was a sure sign of witchcraft, yet here it seems to have been regarded as a miracle. There was only one woman burned for witchcraft in Ireland in medieval times and that was Dame Alice Kytler's handmaid in Kilkenny. The maid's name was Petronella from Meath, so could she have come from Trim? Following torture, twelve-year-old Petronella was tied to a stake and burned alive in front of a cruel mob as she called in vain for her mistress to come to her aid.

In 1415 part of St Mary's was converted by Sir John Talbot, the king's representative in Ireland, into a private manor house. Talbot had fought the French and succeeded in defeating them. In William Shakespeare's play *Henry VI* the following lines appear: 'Is this the scourge of France? Is this the Talbot so much feared abroad, that with his name the mothers still their babes?' Talbot's coat of arms is inserted in the north wall of the west tower of the building.

In 1717 the building was purchased by one of the two main ladies in Jonathan Swift's life, Esther Johnson, better recalled as 'Stella', for £65. Less than two years later she sold it for £200 – it seems there was Celtic Tiger inflation even then – to her friend Swift, author of *Gulliver's Travels* and rector of Laracor, just south of Trim. Swift was always looking for ways to give Stella funds without directly giving money to her, and he sold the house for a tidy profit less than a year later. Esther is commemorated in a plaque next to Swift's in St Patrick's Cathedral, Dublin.

In the latter half of the eighteenth century Talbot's Castle became the diocesan school for Meath. Arthur Wellesley, the future Duke of Wellington, attended school there, as did

William Rowan Hamilton. A boy genius, Hamilton was able to speak thirteen languages fluently by the age of thirteen. He later became Astronomer Royal for Ireland and is supposed to have first observed the stars from the little balcony on the western side of the school. The house is open for guided tours at certain times.

The walled town of Trim grew up in the shelter and shadow of the castle. The Sheepgate is the only surviving medieval gate of Trim's original five gates, which allowed access to the town. On the north bank of the Boyne, the remains of the gate consist of a semi-circular headed arch, which appears to have been surmounted by a tower. The walls kept out the rebel Irish, and tolls and taxes on produce for the local fairs were collected

The remains of the Sheepgate.

at the gates. The other gates were Navangate (on the road to Navan), Athboygate, Dublingate (on Emmet Street, not to be confused with the castle's Dublingate) and Watergate. Watergate protected a crossing on the river.

Situated just outside the town walls, the Black Friary at Trim was founded in 1263 by Geoffrey de Geneville and his wife, Maude. In 2010 the Irish Archaeology Field School commenced a long-term programme of archaeological excavation at the Black Friary site. Excavation has been carried out by a team that includes local people, Irish students from all over the country and international students from all over the world. The archaeological dig (accessed through Griffin Park, off Haggard Street, beside SuperValu) is visible and the archaeologists are welcoming to visitors. A reconstructed medieval garden has also been created.

St Patrick's Church of Ireland Cathedral, situated on St Loman Street and dating from 1802, is supposedly on the site of the first church erected in the area, which was founded before Armagh or Canterbury. It was consecrated a cathedral in 1955. Behind the building are the remnants of its fifteenth-century predecessor. Loman, St Patrick's nephew, was assigned by his uncle the task of guarding their boat at the mouth of the Boyne. Patrick was unsure of the response he would receive to his mission and needed to ensure that the boat was ready for a quick escape if necessary. Loman waited forty days and forty nights, a very biblical number, then waited a further forty, before deciding to venture upstream. The furthest he could go was the ford of Trim. He made camp and the following morning, while saying his daily prayers, a young boy came upon him and, hearing the prayers, asked to be baptised. Instantly believing in Christianity sounds like a miracle, but the little boy was actually the son of a

British princess who was married to the high king's son who had a fort at Trim. This boy had probably been raised by his mother as a Christian; it is known that there were Christians in Ireland before St Patrick's arrival. The street name, St Loman Street, commemorates this first saint to visit Trim.

The church tower of the cathedral probably dates to about 1450 and the clock is the Dean's Clock, recalling the historian of Trim, Dean Richard Butler.

In 1584 local parson Robert Draper recommended Trim as the site for the first university in Ireland, pointing out its many advantages. However, his proposal was not acted upon and eight short years later Trinity College was founded in Dublin.

St Loman Street had a previous name, Scarlet Street. In the eighteenth and nineteenth centuries this was reputedly a violent area and the name was believed to come from the colour of the blood which ran down the middle following fights. The name possibly had another origin – the red coats of the British Army. This street was in a poor area and many men joined the army to make a living. Even during the First World War many of Trim's casualties came from this street.

Scarlet Street had a reputation for being rough well back into history. It is alleged that when St Patrick came on his missionary journey to Trim the people told him they already had one saint, Loman, and did not need a second. Patrick, on his way out of town, passed up Scarlet Street. It was early in the morning and a woman was cleaning out her house. In a good area it was usual to look left and right before throwing something out the door, but clearly in Scarlet Street you kept your head in. The woman, who was emptying a chamber pot, just threw its contents out the door, all over Patrick! He, being a saint, let on that it did not bother him and continued on his way. About a mile out of town Patrick realised that because of the incident he had forgotten to bestow his usual blessing on the settlement. However, he decided the best thing to do was keep going and, not even turning around, he blessed Trim with the back of his hand. A mile outside the town, on the left-hand side of Navan road, the Church of the Back, Kilcooley, commemorates this event.

Thankfully, nowadays the town is much more civilised. In fact it won the Tidy Towns competition in 1972, 1974 and 1984, and was named as the national winner in the Irish Business against Litter awards in 2011. Castle Street, with its estate cottages and beautiful hanging baskets, is one of the most photographed streets in the town.

Trim also played its part in shaping the lives of well-known historic figures, including the Duke of Wellington and Dean Jonathan Swift. The Duke of Wellington's association with the town is commemorated in a Corinthian column that dominates the traffic junction at the top of Emmet Street. The column is 23 metres high and the inscription reads: 'This column was erected in the year 1817 in honour of the illustrious Duke of Wellington by the grateful contributions of the people of Meath.' It was erected on this site as Wellington resided nearby while serving as member of parliament for Trim. No one is sure where exactly Wellington was born; he himself did not know. His generally accepted date of birth is 1 May 1769, the same year which saw the birth of his opponent, Napoleon Bonaparte. His birthplace is less easy to pinpoint – some suggest the family's townhouses in Trim, Athy or Merrion Square, Dublin, or various other houses in Dublin or near Trim. In the 1970s a local historian produced a list of sixteen possible birthplaces, but following a conference

Flowers on Castle Street.

in the 1990s more claims emerged to bring the number closer to thirty. The most likely places are Dublin or Dangan, the family home south of Trim, or perhaps in a coach in between, which may have given rise to his reputed saying: 'To be born in a stable does not make one a horse', meaning to be born in Ireland did not make one Irish, although a real Irishman would never say such a thing about good horseflesh – or would he? No one actually knows who first said this phrase, but it is now thought to have been Daniel O'Connell, who continued: 'It could make him an ass.'

Wherever he was born, we do know that Wellington received

his early education in Talbot's Castle in the eighteenth century. A story goes that one of the duke's schoolmates, Richard Crosbie, climbed to the top of the nearby Yellow Steeple. At the top he took out a piece of a paper and wrote his will in case he fell on the way down, throwing it to the ground. When he arrived safely at the bottom he found young Wellington crying. Crosbie told him not to be afraid – he was down safely. However, Wellington told him that he was actually crying because Crosbie had not left him any of his toys or playthings in the will!

Locals have a love/hate relationship with Wellington and his column. A proposal from a decade ago suggested giving the column to the city of Wellington in New Zealand. A supposed suggestion from an IRA activist to blow up the column, as had happened to Nelson's Pillar in Dublin, was vetoed when it was realised that the nearby pub might suffer damage if an explosion was carried out.

A mile downstream from the town of Trim the first Norman bishop of the diocese of Meath, Simon de Rochfort, founded his cathedral at Newtown in 1206. The largest cathedral in medieval Ireland, constructed in an early Gothic style, the church was assigned into the care of the Victorine friars of the adjoining monastery and dedicated to Saints Peter and Paul. Only a portion of the original nave and chancel of the cathedral survive, as do some walls of the Victorine abbey, which stand between the cathedral and the Boyne.

Surrounding the cathedral ruins is Newtown graveyard. Located within the graveyard are the ruins of the small medieval parish church of Newtown, well worth a visit to see the late-sixteenth-century tomb of Sir Lucas Dillon and his wife, Lady Jane Bathe, inside the church. Known locally as the 'Tomb of the

The remains of the cathedral at Newtown.

The Tomb of the Jealous Man and Woman.

Jealous Man and Woman', the effigies portray Sir Lucas and his wife in Elizabethan dress with a sword dividing the couple. The name of the tomb appears to have come from the fact that the two figures do not touch and the sword separates them.

This tomb is associated with a cure for warts. Rub a pin on a wart, place the pin between the couple on the tomb and as the pin rusts and decays so the wart will disappear. But be warned – if you take a pin from the grave as a keepsake, you will get the warts of the person who left it there!

If you cross back to the south side of the river using the stone bridge that lies just past this site, you will find the remains of a priory and hospital founded in the thirteenth century by an order originally established to nurse the Crusaders and redeem Christian hostages. Wearing a cross on their tunic they became identified as the Crossed or Crutched Friars.

Heading back into town on the Dublin road, just opposite the Victorine priory is the Echo Gate. This is nothing much to look at, but if you shout across the river to the ruined Victorine friary, your voice should return in a perfectly clear echo.

To the south of the town, on the Summerhill road, is the site of Laracor Church. The original building was demolished in 1850 and replaced by a new church, now a private residence. Jonathan Swift was rector in Laracor from 1700 until his death in 1745. One Sunday Swift was to have goose for dinner. When someone in the kitchen tore off one of the goose's legs and ate it, the serving maid was in a quandary and asked the cook what she should do. The cook replied that Swift always had his nose stuck in a book and would not even notice. Eventually convinced, the maid brought the goose up to the waiting diner. Swift looked up and asked the obvious question: 'Why has my goose got only one leg?' The maid thought quickly and, knowing that Swift was a city boy born within the shadows of Dublin Castle, replied, 'That is the South Meath goose and they only have one leg.' Swift, not knowing much about farmyard birds, did not argue. A few days later, while out driving with his coachman, he came upon a gaggle of geese asleep in a field. Geese sleep standing on one leg with the other tucked up under their wing. The coachman, aware of the story of the one-legged goose and possibly the culprit, pointed out the birds to the dean as examples of the South Meath goose. But when he cracked his whip, the geese put down their second leg and flew away. Swift then complained that his goose had not produced its second leg, but the coachman

The Friary of the Crossed or Crutched Friars.

explained that the dean had not cracked a whip at his bird. This is a good story and certainly told about Swift, although a similar story was also told about a bishop of Limerick thirty years before Swift was born.

Further out the Summerhill road is Dangan estate, identified by an obelisk in a field on the right, which was the boyhood home of the Duke of Wellington.

Index

M

N

O

P

R

S

T

U

W